Living
with
Preschoolers

For my friend, Mike,
with my fondest regards —

Willard

11/76

Living with Preschoolers

from the terrible Twos...
to the fascinating Fives!

by

Willard Abraham, Ph.D.

 O'SULLIVAN WOODSIDE & CO.

Illustrated by James Hargis
Cover artwork by Mia Wingfield, age 6

Published in the
United States of America by
O'Sullivan, Woodside & Company,
Phoenix, Arizona, and
simultaneously in Canada by
George J. McLeod, Limited,
Toronto, Ontario.

Manufactured in the
United States of America.

First Edition.

Library of Congress Cataloging in Publication Data

Abraham, Willard.
    Living with preschoolers.

    1. Children—Management. 2. Education, Preschool—
United States. 3. Child development. I. Title.
HQ774.A23   649'.123   76-12645
ISBN 0-89019-055-0

O'SULLIVAN
WOODSIDE
& COMPANY
2218 East Magnolia
Phoenix, Arizona 85034

For
Eddie,
Andy,
Amy
and their Mother
from whom
I've learned
so much.

Contents

Foreword

Having known and worked professionally with the author for more than twenty-five years, it is without hesitation that I recommend this book to parents, teachers and all who live and work with young children.

Dr. Abraham has confidence in parents. He wants to help them increase their understanding of how to guide their children and of their children's needs.

As an educator, father of three children and a leader in the community, he is well-qualified to do all this. Much of his energy is used in working for the rights of children at the local, state and national levels. *Living with Preschoolers* is filled with down-to-earth and interestingly written material which is concerned with everyday situations in the lives of the family team.

This is a book to which you will turn again and again.

DR. FRANCES R. HORWICH

Former "Miss Frances" of
television's *Ding Dong School*

Living
with
Preschoolers

1.

The Young Children in Your Family

"Terrible Twos" . . .
"Trusting Threes" . . .
"Frustrating Fours" . . .
"Fascinating Fives" . . .

An educational series of films some years ago used those terms to describe young children. They were convenient, but often they were way off base.

Anybody who has lived with little ones—in either a home or preschool setting—knows how unpredictable they are, and how faulty such labels can be.

Is he* really "terrible" at two? Not always. Not when he washes his hands and brushes his teeth as you do, when he thinks the whole world is a big joke as he bends over and looks at it upside down between his legs, or when he tries to imitate your whistling, throwing a ball, or piling up blocks.

He likes rough-and-tumble as well as quiet time looking through a picture book with you, helping in the kitchen, water play, and feeding himself (as messy as it might be!).

It isn't always fun-and-games for either you or the two-year-old, of course. It can't be, when he clings,

*Let's not worry about sexism! Of course, we are referring to both boys and girls most of the time when we use "he."

whines, keeps getting out of bed, and has all kinds of fears related to being alone, wet or in the dark.

And how "trusting" is the three-year-old who sometimes has a huge pack of worries? He may be concerned about dogs, death, people who look "odd," hurting himself, or why he (or she) is "made differently" from a sister (or brother). His anxieties can often be handled by a parent who isn't tired or tense, but many times they strain the basic trust most three-year-olds have in adults.

The three-year-old can also be fun and easy to be with. He likes familiar stories read again and again, repetition of nursery rhymes and songs, and make-believe playmates and animals.

When a youngster is four he can be "frustrating," of course, with his "No" and "I won't," his lying without meaning to, and alibis, and bossiness. But he's not always frustrating by any means, as he talks more, listens more and takes care of himself better than when he was two or three. At four he's interested in how things work, action stories and imitating his family, community workers, and television characters.

The five-year-old's independence, broadening interests and dependability are "fascinating" to watch as they emerge from the baby years. But all the home and school relationships aren't calm and placid. Mild deceptions, rivalry, and fears may be part of his life too.

These facts of early childhood add up to a few basic rules for parent-child understanding:

1. Although it is "normal" for children to do all the things mentioned above, the child you live with may deviate by months, or skip whole stages, and still be completely normal. "Normal" isn't a point or moment; it's a spread or range, and sometimes pretty wide too.

2. Perhaps he can't pronounce his "r's" ("wabbit"

comes out instead of "rabbit"), sometimes stutters, misplaces toys, can't thread a needle—but it's seldom anything to worry about at two or three. What should be a basis for parental concern at ten or twelve is rarely a problem when a child is young.

3. The one thing we can be sure of with young children (and older ones too) is that the unexpected is likely to happen.

A problem we often have is that we just don't listen to them enough. We're too busy talking, planning, and directing, too concerned about our own image, or our adult worries of job, inflation and health, or the TV, company or movie we'll be involved in tonight.

We can guide children by using all of their senses, and we can learn about them through all of ours, but it takes a little time and practice.

2.

It's a Different Kind of "School"

Why is your child in a preschool program?

Perhaps you have a job—or there are no other youngsters where you live—or it'll be good for him—or your friends' kids are in one.

What do you really want him to get out of it?

Your expectations make sense to you, even though you probably didn't have this opportunity when you were young. In those days people didn't realize how much intelligence is developed by the time a child is five.

A healthy, early childhood program isn't just a baby sitting service—nor is it like the orderly classroom of your first school experience. When you visit you can expect to see a lot of activities going on at one time. Even though it may sometimes seem noisy and confused, there is a plan at work. It is based on clear-cut objectives, like these:

Learning about himself. He is finding out that he can plan something and follow through, whether it's connected with block building, painting, cutting and pasting, or taking care of himself at meals or in the bathroom. He is learning that he can understand books, listen to records, set the table, and help select field trips to make or seeds to plant. He knows that he is getting bigger and stronger. He begins to see that he can get along with other children, and is finding out that he has changing likes and dislikes in food, toys and games.

Getting ready for reading. A child really begins to learn to read in infancy, when he starts to differentiate between bright red and pale pink, dull pablum and a delicious apricot flavor, his mother and everyone else. Such early differences are sharpened and refined during the two-to-five years. He hears stories, acts them out, and talks about them. A youngster gets ready to read by saying and understanding more words, going more places, and seeing more things. The increasing ability to express himself and to listen to what you say relates directly to how well he will soon interpret pages in a book.

Developing his senses. Although most of what all of us have learned came through our eyes, we missed a lot. The other senses—hearing, touch, taste, and smell—can stimulate a child to learn a great deal about himself and the world around him. When are shapes the same or different? What do words like "right," "left," "up," "down," "in," "out" and "around" mean? How can the textures of burlap, velvet, and sandpaper be described? All these help a child grow up when they are talked about with a teacher who listens, who makes a youngster feel important, and who encourages conversation.

Contributing to physical development. Most of us can't afford smooth slides, safe swings, bars, pulleys, balance beams or other creative equipment that contribute toward the development of large muscles. Nor do we have the time and patience to encourage small muscle development through matching, measuring, collecting, putting puzzles together, stringing beads and building with small blocks, sticks and stones. But these child settings do all that, and much more.

That's only the beginning of what you'll see in many well-operated day care/child care/nursery schools/preschools.

They teach numbers through enjoyable counting games, getting your youngster ready for arithmetic.

They help him understand that he can't always have his own way, and. that tantrums, grabbing and screaming don't pay off. Their teachers still accept and love him, but they show that they don't necessarily like what he does, through their calm, fair, firm handling rather than through adult anger.

They teach safety with toys, in a tree, and on the street, and how to get along peacefully with others, listen quietly, and express his ideas so that others understand.

These preschools carry quite a load that helps pave the way toward better learning at school and easier living at home.

3.

The P/P/P
Parent-Preschool Partnership

When you send your child off to a nursery school, preschool or child or day care center, do you ever have a guilty feeling?

A lot of parents do, whether their reason for enrolling him is so that they can go to work or just to have some free time.

A good way to look at the situation is as a partnership in which you and the center are both involved for the youngster's benefit. No matter how long your child is there each day, you remain as the "senior partner" with the major responsibility for guiding and shaping him into the kind of person you want him to be. However, their personnel can be very helpful if the two-way communication between home and school is kept open.

Here are three of the most important areas in which it can be put to work:

Getting along with other children. The preschool can tell you who his best friends are, which toys he enjoys sharing with others and which he likes to play with alone, and any concerns they have about his being bossy or shy and what they are trying to do about them.

You can let them know what difficulties you have in arranging for him to be with other youngsters (because of your work schedule, where you live, or other reasons), the kinds of social or solitary play situations, toys and equipment available to him at home and in your neighborhood, and how he acts with children when you observe him.

You and they can compare how he performs at home and in school. Sharing your information and theirs can help both of you follow up on what the other is doing.

Developing language skills. From the day care/pre-school you can find out how his vocabulary and speech patterns compare with those of other children his age. They can fill you in on what they are doing to develop them, through telling about and acting out stories and talking about plans for the painting, music, counting, meal, playground and other activities scheduled in sound child centers.

What you can do at home to supplement their work may consist of reading to him, talking about his day's events, and mainly doing what comes so hard to most adults—*listening to what he has to say.*

If they tell you about his specific language and speech strengths and weaknesses (and what they are doing to capitalize on or eliminate them), their approach will give you an idea of what you can do in the time you have him at home. And when you tell them you are worried about how he pronounces certain words ("yady" for "lady," for example), they can indicate whether that's normal for his age or really a problem.

Accepting responsibilities. Well-organized preschools don't just talk about helping your youngster become more responsible. They move that objective into action as the child puts toys away, gets into and out of clothing, cleans up the watercoloring area, arranges the table for lunch, helps plan the little garden or window box plants, and feeds the goldfish, mice, rabbits or gerbils. The school can supervise such activities, but they can't—and shouldn't—have the sole responsibility for helping him grow up.

The "senior partner" has to follow through with the toys, dressing, clean up, table setting, planning, and animals (if there are any) at home. The teacher and her aides can tell you what to expect (a two-year-old putting away *one* toy is something to be pleased with, for instance) and what they are working on at the preschool to help your child accept responsibilities appropriate to his age and development. You can share with them any particular skills you'd like them to work on that are important to you and your family.

They don't have your youngster for the whole day, evening and weekends, and neither do you. If you aren't aware of what play and work activities the school is involved in and they don't know what needs and concerns you feel, your child may not get the most out of what can be a rich experience.

This parent-preschool partnership can provide a solid foundation for later school success and home adjustment. Through it you will obtain a clear picture of what your youngster is capable of doing now and where his potential abilities and problems lie.

4.

What Kind of Parent Am I?

"How effective am I as a parent?"

Do you ever ask yourself that question? Perhaps you do, and your answer may be "So-so," "Pretty bad" or even "Great!"

Here is a self-rating scale that may help you look at yourself a little more objectively. It will just take a few minutes to complete. On a separate sheet of paper, score yourself:

Good—2 points; Fair—1; Poor—0; I don't know—?

1. *Communication.* Young children try to use a lot of words, but not always accurately, nor are they always easy to understand. But correcting them isn't as important as listening, exchanging ideas, and actually carrying on a conversation. Do I let them tell me what they did at their day care center or preschool? Do we have some "Talking Time" every day? Do I answer their questions, in words they can understand?

2. *Time.* Merely spending time together is less important than enjoying or laughing at things together. Do we really like each other's company? Do I regularly take time for playing a game, taking a walk, going to the park or seeing a movie with my preschool child?

3. *Example.* Children learn by copying their parents. Do I set a good example by following through on my job, being honest in my relationships, and showing moderation in my TV watching, drinking, eating, sleeping and other habits? Nibbling grapes from the supermarket fruit bin may seem like such a small thing, but it's too important to be seen by a young child. What kind of example do I set in controlling my temper and moodiness?

4. *Expectations and responsibilities.* Are the expectations I have for my children realistic—or too high or low? Do they help with the dishes, make beds, pick up clothes, and do other home chores of which they are capable? Do I add to their duties gradually? Is my preschool child beginning to understand money and what things cost?

5. *Praise.* Do I use praise, or just nag? Do I notice and reward (even with a kind word) what my young child does, whether it's something small like taking out the garbage or a big achievement like reading his first word in a book?

6. *Limitations.* Do our family rules fit the age and abilities of my children? Do I set limits that make sense for each child, like a time for going to bed or the amount of TV watching permitted? But do I also realize that there has to be some flexibility in schedules, to help children adjust to change?

7. *Reading.* Do my young children see me reading, and do I read to them? Is it fun for them and me? Do we choose the books together, and have a good time talking about them? How often do I go to the library with them?

8. *Strengths and Weaknesses.* Do I make an effort to see my children as they really are, not as I'd like them to be? Do I accept the fact that they may not be as good-looking and clever as I sometimes think they are? Am I aware of their limitations, as in catching a ball, cutting with a scissors, skipping or hopping? If they are lagging behind others, am I doing something about it?

9. *Discipline.* If we are a two-parent family, do we agree on approaches to discipline? Do we stick together in our ideas so that our children can't play one of us against the other? If I'm the only parent, am I consistent in the discipline I use? Do I try to prevent problems by keeping medicines, candy, and valuable breakable things away from little hands?

10. *Love.* It's the most important factor of all. Do I try to show it through buying them everything they ask for—or in more important ways like hugs, touching, smiles, quiet talk, and saying nice things?

Well, how did you do? A perfect score would be 20, and if you ended up with 16 to 20 points, that may sound fine—but one item you failed on may be enough to mess up your whole relationship. For example, if you never use praise or use it dishonestly, or think that showing your love is a sign of weakness, it may not matter at all how well you did on the others.

Still, a high score . . . and a low score, too . . . may tell you something about your parental effectiveness. These items can also be a guide toward a better understanding of your youngster, and of yourself.

And a lot of "I don't know's" say something important to you too, like, "Maybe it's time to think more about the young child in my family."

5.

Helping Your Child Get Ready to Read

Can you help your preschool child get ready to read? Is it worthwhile?

Can it contribute to, rather than interfere with, the actual teaching of reading later on in school?

The answer is yes, to all three questions.

This enjoyable experience for you and your youngster requires no special preparation and very little time.

What you can do is based on three items, and your child already has a strong start in all of them:

1. Listening
2. Seeing
3. Words

Some fancy educational labels say almost the same thing:

1. Auditory discrimination and memory
2. Visual discrimination and memory
3. Vocabulary or language development.

Stated more simply, they add up to giving him greater experience with the *sounds, sights* and *words* that are all around him every day.

Here are just a few examples of the many activities through which you can help him get ready to read. If you ask your youngster's preschool teacher you will no doubt get many additional suggestions.

Listening

• *Following instructions.* Start with one, and gradually add others. Does he pay attention while you're talking? Does he stick with a job until it's finished? Do you tell him how well he did it?

• *Sounds.* Ask him, "What sound does a snake (or train, plane or sheep) make?" "Close your eyes, and make the same sound I make (p...b...m...s...t...d)." "Do these words sound the same? . . . Or how are they different?" (Examples are "boy . . . toy," "rug . . . hug," "see . . . me ").

• *Hearing games.* Remind him that it may seem perfectly quiet, but there are sounds around us. "What do you hear?" Or ask him, with his eyes closed, "Tell me what you heard." (Drop the keys, slam a door, run water, type, use the vacuum cleaner.) "What word rhymes with . . . ?" (Use common ones like "rose," "cat," "tree," and "cow.")

Seeing

• *Eye test.* Have his eyes examined by a competent person. This is a basic step in getting him ready to read.

• *Missing items.* Put out three or four (like a pencil, button, eraser, spoon), ask him to close his eyes, and then remove one. "Which one is missing?" Have him shut his eyes while you rearrange them. "Put them as they were before."

• *Comparisons.* Use blocks, beads, pictures or magnetized letters on your refrigerator. "How are they the same (different)?" "Which is bigger (or smaller, most, least, above, below, on, under, next to, inside, outside, behind)?" Use buttons, nails and pieces of cloth to get at comparisons in shapes, sizes, colors and textures.

• *Drawing, puzzles, directions, copying.* Say to him, "That's a pretty tree (or big truck). Can you draw it?"

Encourage him to color within boundaries and to draw a line between other lines (straight, curved and angled) without touching them. Use cut-up pictures of faces, animals or cars; puzzles are fun to put together. "Show me which way the auto is going (or the lady is facing)." "Can you put these beads on a string as I do? Let's try."

Words

• *Games.* Ask him, "What will happen if it rains today, (Andy or Amy comes over to play, we stick a pin in a balloon, or we plant these seeds)?"

• *Books.* Read to him, even if it's for only a few minutes a day. Use the local library, taking him along. Buy some books with lots of pictures and a few words. Help him notice that they have pages that go from front to back, top to bottom, and left to right. Ask him, "How do you think this story ends?" As you go along, ask specific questions like, "What did the boy want?" and "What was the girl wearing?" Have him mention objects or events in illustrations that are also in the book.

• *Pictures.* Use them from television commercials, billboards, and grocery cans, asking "What is it called?" "How do you think this happened?" (a wrecked car in a newspaper picture), "What is this? What caused it?" (a flood), "What do we have to do to get some?" (beautiful flowers). Such questions can help increase young vocabularies.

Don't feel you have to use all of these ideas—or that these are the only ones to use. A few may go a long way for you and your youngster. Too many questions and boredom are signs that you might be trying too hard.

It's important to keep your eye on the right target—to increase your preschool child's *listening, seeing* and *word* experiences. That goal can become a sound basis for competent and enjoyable reading in all the school years that lie ahead.

6.

The Young Child's Eating and Meals
Pleasure or Problem?

You are what you eat, say some people. And the adult your child will become depends to an important degree on what he eats in his youngest years.

Many of us fight our adult battle of overweight and cholesterol, of wrong foods, overeating and poor meal schedules. However, there are some easy ways to help your young child get off to a better start. Here are six of them:

• Recognize that the amount a child should eat depends on his appetite, size, and tendency to put on weight. Although you should choose *what* he eats, let him decide on *how much*.

• Understand that each child has food likes and dislikes just as we do, so why not try to appeal to his tastes? Supermarket and grocery store shelves provide a lot of variety these days, although it's necessary, of course, to keep costs in mind.

• Provide between-meal snacks, but they needn't be just candy, sweet cookies, potato chips and soft drinks. A regular snacktime based on milk, fruit juice, raw vegetables, dry cereals, and dry or fresh fruit is healthful. Besides, most children like them.

• Encourage your youngster to eat what is "good for him" through small servings, mild seasoning, separate foods (most youngsters don't like casseroles, and they do like divided plates), colorful foods (like gelatins and pieces of parsley), and various textures (chewy, crisp and soft, rather than all the same).

• Make it all easier for his little fingers and hands. Soup in a cup, small bite-size pieces, and food that can be picked up often help cut down on mealtime nagging, yelling and jangled nerves. (By the way, so can plastic dishes, washable floor coverings and chairs to match children's sizes.)

• Try to schedule meals that don't last too long and at times when youngsters are rested. That may help reduce the tension many of us face after a tough day's work, fighting traffic, or figuring out how to pay the expanding family bills. We need a calm mealtime as much as they do—perhaps more!

Preschoolers often go through stages of wanting to dictate what, where and when they will eat, and that's normal. Maybe his eating alone or earlier will help solve that problem, for no member of the family really has the right to spoil it for everyone else.

Getting all the main elements into the daily diet is less difficult than it may seem at first. It used to be rigidly recommended that so much milk, fruit, vegetables, meat, bread and cereals were needed every day, but now the recommendation is simpler.

A child from two to five years old needs 25 to 30 grams of protein and 1250 to 1600 calories a day.

Here are some sample protein and calorie figures:

	Protein (grams)	Calories
One glass of milk (whole)	9	160
One egg	6	80

One ounce of meat (for example, beef)	7	80
One ounce of cheese (for example, American)	7	105
A dish of ice cream	2	95
A raw carrot	1	20
Mashed potatoes	2	93
A banana	1	100

Giving a child too much protein is costly and nutritionally wasteful. It is better to fill the rest of his diet with foods he likes that are light in both protein and fats.

A government pamphlet entitled *Nutritive Value of Foods* goes into far more detail on all major foods. If you'd like a copy write to the Superintendent of Documents, U.S. Government Printing Office, Washington, D.C. 20402. It has a lot of advice for weight-conscious, calorie-counting adults too.

Now, for a last, kind of touchy point. Our children learn a great deal from us, and if we are the chocolate, chewing gum, popcorn, rich ice cream type, why should we expect them to be different? If we steadily nibble sweets and have an irregular meal schedule, why be surprised if they do too? If we enjoy foods that are fried or heavy in fats, perhaps we should cut down a bit, for the sake of our own heart as well as for our children's health.

After all, we are the most important teacher they will ever have through the example we set every day.

Your youngster's health and ability to learn are directly related to what he eats—and it's never too early to get the right habits started.

7.

Discipline and Punishment
Where Do You Stand?

He took the hose and pumped water into the gas tank of your new car.

    ... ran into the street and was almost hit.

    ... tried to hide a key in the electrical wall plug.

    ... pulled up all the violets you just planted.

    ... let the bird out of the cage.

    ... cut his friend's hair (and his friend cut his).

    ... ran away.

What do you do about situations like these? Which side are you on: (1) A hard walloping, regardless of the offense, is the best and only appropriate punishment; (2) there is never a reason to hit a young child; (3) other kinds of punishment are often more effective.

Parents usually punish a child to prevent danger to him or destruction of something that belongs to him or others. Sometimes it's just to release their own tensions.

A sound approach to discipline should include more than stopping a youngster from doing what you don't want him to do. Severe physical punishment given in anger may teach a child something you didn't intend, that temper tantrums and hitting are acceptable behavior—as long as an adult hands it out.

The purpose of discipline is to help a child learn to behave in a desirable, safe way, and to respect the property and feelings of others. It is to direct him toward what he can do, where he can ride his bike, dig holes, and pound pots and pans, rather than where he can't.

A young child generally wants to please his parents. He is seldom "bad" deliberately. You can help him do the "right" thing if you expect him to, and if you tell him how well he puts his things away, gets ready for bed, and brushes his teeth. Your smiles, approval and love are very important to him.

Here are ten common sense guidelines to discipline. Perhaps they can help prevent problems and useless punishment with your own preschool child.

- Discipline and punishment are not the same thing. A well-disciplined child may seldom have to be punished. Learning right from wrong can frequently come through your patient explanations, your own carefulness (crossing streets, using tools, and shutting car doors, for example), and temporarily depriving him of something he wants.
- He needs limits and controls. Young children can't handle total freedom. But they should have the chance to create, experiment, and make simple decisions.
- Spankings and yelling may sometimes be avoided if you use "preventative discipline." Problems with valuable breakables, medicines, and hot soup on the front burner can all be prevented. Besides, they aren't as much fun as washable crayons (and an acceptable place to use them), blocks that fit together, and a colorful book you read to him.
- Children usually behave better when they are busy, and not so well when they are bored or tired.
- No single set of rules or punishment fits all children. The shy, quiet child needs encouragement to open up, and parental strictness may be a mistake. But for the secure, outgoing one a few rules and restrictions,

carefully developed and clearly understood, may provide important guidance.

- You can confuse a young child if you offer choices when the decision should be yours. "Do you want to eat (or go to bed)?" gives him a chance to say, "No!" And then you might get into the "Yes-you-will-no-I-won't" routine.

- Harsh punishment may be remembered—but not the reason for it. Endless scoldings, the silent treatment and shame and ridicule are generally not very effective with young children. Words and looks are sometimes enough to show your disapproval.

- Occasionally there are good reasons for changing the rules. More important than nap-time may be what he's doing right at that moment. Respect for his interests can help avoid conflicts between you and him.

- Some of the best discipline comes in his relationships with others. He will learn that being selfish about toys and hitting friends doesn't pay off; they'll just play with others or go home.

- Your expectations should be realistic. We sometimes forget that it takes more than two to five years to learn all the rules of safety, respect for others, and self-control.

One additional factor is important. With all the pressures you face every day, perhaps you can't always be as calm as you might like to be. It is good for your children to learn early to "roll with" your moods and needs just as you try to adjust to theirs. That ability is also part of good discipline.

8.

The Single-Parent Family

Mother, father and home are the young child's whole world. But neither divorce nor separation will necessarily destroy it.

The single parent has to hold it together, and most parents left to live alone with one or more children have all that is needed to create a well-adjusted, healthy family unit.

Although the religious factor dominates this situation for some people, for most of them their personal desires, needs and "How will our children be affected?" take top consideration.

Having two parents around is of course important, but it's not essential. More significant may be the fact that tension, hostility or indifference might also leave when one parents walks out. That closing door may even bring a sense of relief, with quiet and peacefulness at home for the first time.

There are all kinds of "broken homes," and whether yours is really wrecked, temporarily cracked, or perhaps even more solid depends on the strength of the parent left behind, the help of family and friends, and the ability to ease children through the change. It also depends on how well the practical burdens of money, sickness and discipline are handled. (Separation through death of a parent often provides additional emotional burdens, of course.)

A preschool child living with one parent is frequently troubled inwardly. "I did it ... they blame me. . . they don't love me" are feelings that can lead to anger, fear and resentfulness. He may not actually say these things, but he could feel them deeply.

They sometimes come out through hard-to-handle eating, sleeping and bathroom habits, fights with brothers, sisters and friends, biting and scratching, and belligerence toward naps and other routines that ran so smoothly until the family broke up.

How well your young child adjusts to the separation can relate to your using approaches like these:

• Recognize that keeping the separation secret, once it is firmly decided on, merely increases anxiety and puzzlement. But a small child doesn't need much time to accept an empty place at meal-time.

• Help him see that he wasn't the reason for it, that it's between two adults and not because of him. It is important for him to realize that you both love him, so *say* it and *show* it.

• Control as much as possible any bitterness you may feel, so that his distress can be reduced at least a little bit. A young child is very sensitive to bickering, loud arguments and long silences. He can't handle them in loneliness and fear.

• Try to keep alive his love for the other parent.

• Don't use your child as an emotional outlet or as a "replacement." "You're now the man of the house" may be satisfying and flattering at first, but children shouldn't be expected to provide a substitute for adult affection and companionship to fill the single parent's empty hours. If you need an outlet, seek another adult.

• Recognize that more time and listening may be necessary, but don't assume you have to carry this responsibility so far that friends and hobbies must be restricted or eliminated. You need them too.

If you have to move, let him keep as many familiar toys and possessions as possible. And if you're getting ready to remarry, realize that children need time to "make friends" with a new parent.

One of the most valuable sources of help to the single-parent family which includes a young child is a competently run nursery school or preschool. It's vital to check out its personnel, program and facilities.

If you tell them about your situation, they can help compensate for whatever family deficiencies might exist. People he can love, friends he needs, and toys and large equipment are all available there.

Your adjustment rubs off on your children. If you can live comfortably within your budget, be satisfied with your job, and adapt to being single reasonably well, you generally have little to worry about as far as your youngsters are concerned. They can accept both change and sacrifice when the need is obvious, and when you set the example of taking them in stride.

34

9.

Every Child is Creative

Children lose part of their creativity by the time they are five. That's what some of the research says.

But do they really have to? Can you do something to help your youngsters retain the curiosity, eagerness to explore and learn, and imagination of their first few years?

Yes, you certainly can. And it costs very little in time and money.

Because a child's areas of enjoyment are so numerous, many parents get scared off, however. "What do I know about animals, gardening and magnets?... I'm a dud at music, dancing and art.... Let the schools do it."

What parents can do to encourage creativity isn't really difficult. Here are a few samples:

• Young children like to use their bodies—jump, rock, dance, sway, creep, skip and walk in funny ways—using their heads, hands, arms and legs. Let music come into your house through records, radio, television or instruments.

• Young children like to make things, sometimes using tools and brushes. They like to feel different materials, and squeeze them through their fingers. Once in a while provide clay, scraps of soft wood, colored paper, and even paint, sand and mud. It'll all wash off! Some items aren't safe and some stain, so that's where your adult judgment has to come in.

• Young children like to make believe. Give them the puppets, grown-up clothes, and other props out of which they'll create a whole new world of magic and fantasy. You might be an audience for them occasionally—and you might even enjoy the show.

• Young children like to rhyme sounds and words, tell stories, and compose songs and poems. Encourage them—and once in a while leave the TV or newspaper and listen to them. Use waiting moments in grocery stores, doctors' offices and traffic delays, and don't be too upset with what may seem like silly behavior. If they can't "let themselves go" when they're two, three or four, when can they?

A walk in the rain, a seed planted in a window box, a magnifying glass, a thank-you letter to grandma, a castle made with blocks—ideas for creative growth are all around us.

They extend to your own interest areas too. Young children like nothing better than to be included in your activities and hobbies, even if it's cooking, auto repair, or carpentry.

Three cautions are important: (1) Let's not be "sexist" (girls can use a hammer, boys may like to play house, and both activities are good starts toward meeting later needs); (2) don't expect too much (preschoolers' sewing may need adult assistance in threading and knot-removing, for example); (3) don't set firm patterns or models for them to follow (it really isn't necessary that they paint within strict lines).

To help children keep and expand the creativity of their early years requires parent understandings like these:

• Recognize that everything is new for them. "Everything" includes the sky, clouds, rain, stars and wind, and extends to tiny insects, pebbles, snowflakes and leaves that most adults seldom notice. After all, small children are often a couple of feet closer to them than we are!

• Accept the idea that the exciting world comes to them through their eyes, but also through sounds, tastes and smells, and by way of their finger tips too.

• Realize that we have to show interest to help them retain theirs, but it's foolish to fake it. Most children, even young ones, are alert to parents acting as though they enjoy childhood games when they're really a bore to them.

• Emphasize that the pictures they draw, the sounds and words they create, and the body movements they make are their very own. They are as much theirs, and theirs alone, as their fingerprints are.

Preschool teachers can provide many additional ideas relating to what your child does on which you can build. If you want to treat yourself to an exciting view of what a young child's world is really like and what you can do to help him retain the way he views the beauty of it as he grows older, locate a copy of Rachel Carson's *The Sense of Wonder* (Harper & Row). All parents of preschool children could benefit from her point of view based on happiness through discovery.

Because some school restrictions may soon close in on your youngster, it's especially important to use these early years which pass so quickly to help establish the habit of creativity.

10.
Brothers and Sisters
Getting Along Together

Quarreling . . . teasing . . . yelling at each other . . . this is the normal situation in most families. Even preschoolers get involved in what seems like a never-ending race to be first, to have the last word, and to get hold of a toy (especially if it belongs to a brother or sister).

Some of your friends may tell you that their children always get along well together. They never argue or fight, really love one another. But they are probably not seeing their children as they really are or they have unusual children.

Most brothers and sisters are in competition with each other. The closer they are in age the more they compete for your affection and approval, and the more they may show resentment when you do something for one and not for the rest.

Young children have an especially difficult time. They may not yet have learned the skill of sharing and "taking turns," or the fun there is in giving as well as receiving.

Some conflict among children can be prevented. Much of it takes place when they are tired, hungry or bored. Touchy periods also occur when they are forced to spend too much time together. Irritants like shared closets, radios and toys aren't always necessary.

Even a major period of stress, like when a new baby comes, can be planned for so that a preschooler doesn't feel displaced or rejected. A little preparation can keep him from asking inwardly, "Wasn't I good enough?"

Sharing the news a few weeks ahead of time, making room changes or preschool arrangements before the baby comes, using the young child as a helper with the baby, and expecting him to slip back into babyish habits (without punishment or ridicule from you) are among the ways you can ease him and you through this period.

A few basic rules of parental common sense can help reduce rivalry among your children:

- Recognize that each child is different. You may give one more time because he requires it, another more compliments (but only earned ones) because he needs them, and a third a particular book, a paint set, or a ball and bat because he will make good use of them.
- Understand that their relationships are affected by their age, place in the family and sex, as well as by their appearance, personality, interests and abilities. For example, the youngest has never been an only child (the oldest was), the middle one is kind of closed in, and one girl among boys (or a boy among girls) is in a position different from all the rest.
- Avoid comparisons. They merely add to possible conflict and tension.
- Make each one special in some way, through time you spend with him or her alone, for example. They all need to feel important, and parents are the best ones to satisfy that need. A good preschool can also help in creating a secure, happy self-image.
- Develop a fair pattern of seniority. Older brothers and sisters may get the comics first and stay up later, but all have to share responsibilities in line with their

maturity (taking out the garbage, straightening up their rooms, caring for pets and other family chores). However, young children can receive special attention; they may be the only ones read to, played with, and taken to the grocery store, all events that are fun for them.

• Encourage respect among all of them (and on your part too) for their privacy and possessions. Even the youngest deserve uninterrupted time to finish a game or build a block castle.

• Keep out of disagreements unless one is always getting the worst of it, and even then only when you know all sides of the problem.

• Realize that all's not lost, not when they are able to present a united front in planning a birthday surprise for you, pull together against the bully down the block, or boast of each other's accomplishments.

• Let their feelings come out, even if they are sometimes noisy. It's better than forcing their resentment and jealousy underground. Let them know their attitudes are normal, just as are the ways in which younger ones admire and imitate and older ones protect and teach.

Perhaps the most important factor related to childhood family rivalry is this: The love and hate, fun and quarrels, and help and hurt are the best foundation for the compromises, adjustments, and competition we all have to face throughout our lives.

11.

Help Your Children Talk Better

No one is able to talk at birth. What young children say and how they say it is learned during their first few years. And they learn mainly by imitation and because they need and want things.

They hear you, their brothers and sisters, and playmates. They find out that they can get a toy or a piece of candy by asking for it.

If parents want to help their children talk better they should speak and listen to them, beginning in infancy and through the preschool years.

For most children speech is acquired in this order: Infancy—sounds and babbling; by one year old—the first words; by two—words combined into simple sentences; by three—sentences and questions.

But some children reach these stages at different times, and they may be just as "normal." Nothing is necessarily wrong because they are a little slower than others are.

Nor do they all learn to speak clearly in these early years. Far from it! Among the sounds that come first and are usually easiest for them are **p, b, m** and **n.** Later come **t, g, d** and **k.** And still later (sometimes not until youngsters are five or six) they may begin to use **l, f, s,** and **r** and combinations like **sh, st, th, tr** and **bl** correctly.

To check out your own young children listen how they pronounce words like "stop," "rabbit," "thumb," "black," "train" and "lady."

Most children do not master all the sounds until they are at least seven or eight years old.

Young children often hesitate, repeat and stumble over their words, but they are probably not "stuttering." Haven't you ever found it difficult to talk smoothly about something important to someone who's not interested? Youngsters frequently face the blank wall of parental disinterest.

It doesn't help to tell them, "You can say it better . . . Try again . . . Talk slowly." It may help a great deal more to talk clearly and calmly yourself, and to avoid as many tense, frustrating situations for them as you can.

To label the normal speech of three and four year olds as "stuttering" could lead to actual stuttering. A child may then need special help for many years to overcome it.

There are several reasons why preschool children do not speak clearly. The main one is that they haven't developed the necessary skills. Two others are baby talk that either you or others think is "cute" and not enough conversation with your youngsters. Less frequent causes of early hard-to-understand speech patterns are hearing problems and poor development of the complicated speech mechanism.

What parents can do about the speech and vocabulary of their preschool youngsters falls into two main parts: (1) You can help prevent difficulties; (2) you can help correct minor ones.

• *Prevention.* Do you let him finish what he wants to say? Do you answer his questions (within reason!)? Do you sometimes try to echo back what he says but in expanded form? (If he says "Shoe" or "More," you might respond, "Yes, your shoe is right here" or "Of course, you can have some more jello.") Do you talk to him in full, short sentences, or just in sharp commands like "Wash your hands," "Eat," "Go to bed" and "Stop that right now!?" Do you really listen to *what* he is saying or just to *how* he says it?

• *Correction of minor difficulties.* Listen for indistinct sounds like "thoap" for "soap" and "fum" for "thumb." You and your youngster can then collect pictures of things that begin with those correct sounds. Say the words accurately and encourage him to do so. Praise him when he does. But try this activity only if you have the patience, and limit yourself to a few minutes a day.

Games based on rhyming words, "What's another way to say—," and "How do you think the story ends?" (when reading to him) are other approaches you can use.

You can help develop correct speech and build vocabulary in these important early years. So can a good preschool or nursery school whose teachers can assist you in expanding on the suggestions offered here.

12.

The Man in Your Young Child's Family

Every young child needs a man in the family. Most little children have one. If there isn't a father, it might be necessary to bring in someone else. Grandfathers, uncles, cousins, older brothers or adult male friends may have to be the father-substitute.

Modern preschools and day care centers try to hire men as teachers or teacher aides. Because few have entered this field, masculine contact generally has to come at home.

It's important for both little boys and girls. They get a strange view of the world around them if they see only women earning a living, paying bills and running the house. Even if their mother reads to them, plays with them, and answers most of their questions, young children still miss something they need very much.

Just any adult male can't fill the gap. He should be one they can look up to and admire, and whose strength and gentleness both come through to them.

But merely "being around" isn't enough either. He must get involved with them, in what they do, think and say. His tasks can be fun, are not difficult, and don't require much time.

The man in your child's family can check himself on these eight factors to see how well he is doing.

• When did you last sit on the floor with the youngster? How often do you do it?

• What do you do with him when you're there? Is it something about which he is excited, that he enjoys and talks about, and in which he wants you to take part?

• Do you listen to him? Do you share your ideas with him so he can understand them? Do you respond to his ideas in words that are clear to him? Do you talk in full sentences?

• What do you do when you first come home from work (or if you're not the father, when you first come in)? For those few minutes, are you willing to put off looking at the newspaper or television and talking to other adults, giving him your full attention? The first five minutes are often more important to young children than all the rest of the evening hours put together.

• Are you willing to let him help you with some of your own jobs around the house? Maybe it will take a few minutes longer that way, but do you let him help fix the faucet, put a battery in a flashlight, or cut the grass? Do you discuss with him what you're doing while you do it?

• How often do you spend time alone with one child, with no other children or adults around? It needn't be a long involvement either, maybe just as simple as taking a walk around the block with him or taking him to the store with you.

• Do you ever hold his hand, let him sit on your lap, hug him, or kiss him? It's far from being a sign of weakness to touch children. You'll like it, and most of them do too.

• Does it bother you that little boys sometimes play with dolls and little girls like to use tools to fix and make things? It isn't really necessary that preschoolers know all about the sex roles they will fill later on. Doing what's expected will probably come in time anyway.

48

Whenever possible the man/child relationship should begin in the earliest months and continue on a regular basis during the preschool years (and later too). If it becomes a special thing—like once a month—it can't be a natural, normal part of a little boy's or girl's life.

Fathers and the adult male substitutes set an example for young children. The little eyes and ears see and hear everything they do. They learn so much by imitating.

The man in your child's family is an important teacher, and it may sometimes be necessary to remind him of that fact. Then, remind him again—and again—how much his little boy or girl needs at least a little of his time, attention, and love.

13.

Learning Disabilities
Some Young Children Have Them

"Learning disabilities" has become a common label for many school-age children. It refers to learning habits that are delayed or seem mixed up or confused. Such problems are often ignored by parents and teachers for too long.

The time for you to notice and start doing something about them (if they really exist) is during the preschool years. But first, you may need a little information:

1. Behavior of some two, three, and four-year-olds that is hard to live with does not necessarily mean that they will have learning problems later on. Immature ways are normal for young children.

2. Just because a youngster takes a little longer than others to learn some things (for example, riding a bike, putting together a puzzle, or learning the rules of a new game) doesn't mean he is "learning disabled." We all learn at different rates.

3. Children who have learning disabilities are usually of average or above-average intelligence. They are definitely *not* mentally retarded.

What seems strange or different to you might not to others who are more objective. Experienced day care and preschool teachers may be your best source for advice.

Here are some characteristics that can help you tell

whether a young child will have learning problems. If he (or she) has one or two of them it may not be important, but a combination of several could be cause for concern.

What to look for
- Is his behavior especially uncontrollable?
- Did he start to walk late? How is his coordination now (like catching a ball or copying or tracing simple designs)? Does he often fall when running?
- Do people outside the family have difficulty in understanding him?
- Does he have a problem finding his toys and clothes even after you tell him many times?
- Does he run off after a few seconds, rather than sticking with a task or game?
- Does he frequently act tired or not interested, or seem to be afraid or worried, in connection with activities that other children enjoy?
- Is it difficult for him to tell sounds apart—a bell from a buzzer, a tap from a clap, or words that rhyme?
- Do a square, a triangle, and a rectangle look the same to him? Can he tell them apart?
- Does he quickly forget what you've shown or told him?
- Is it difficult for him to tell that things feel differently, like various cloths, sand paper and wood, or salt, coffee and sugar? Can he tell one taste or smell from another?
- Is he confused about the difference between up and down, over and under, and outside and inside?
- Does he give the same answer, again and again, to different questions?

What to do
- Reduce distractions. Cut down the clutter and

confusion around him. For example, read to him away from the TV, the telephone and other conversations.

• Help give structure to his young life. Set limits that are reasonable. Be sure he understands them.

• Help him plan ahead. Keep the plans simple. Concentrate on today, not next week. Well-organized time, space, and activities can reduce his confusion.

• Try not to put him "in the middle" between his parents or other adults. Agree in advance about what he will do and when.

• Praise him freely, but don't use fake compliments.

• Encourage him to do things at which he can succeed.

• Involve him in activities that can help him become orderly, like setting the table, putting groceries away, and sorting laundry.

• Have fun with differences and similarities: Sweet and sour *tastes;* various *smells;* textures that *feel* different; colors, sizes and shapes that *look* different; loudness and other variations in *sound.*

• Give him one direction at a time. Use short sentences and simple words.

If he actually is learning disabled, the earlier you discover and help correct the problem the better. School people probably will later on anyway, but why lose valuable time?

14.

Accidents, Safety and Young Children

Each year 15,000 children die in accidents and 700,000 are hurt by toys. One out of every five is injured, maybe even crippled for life.

Will your youngster be one of them this year?

Most accidents—and the pain and tears they cause—can be avoided.

Toys. Parents sometimes forget the main rules of toy safety: (1) Almost any toy can be unsafe if a child is too young for it or doesn't know how to use it; (2) all toys should be checked for loose, broken, missing and rusty parts; (3) ones not put away might be tripped on—and it isn't only children who fall over them!

Button eyes on dolls, tiny wheels and other small parts too often end up in throats, ears and noses. Just as dangerous can be the wires, pins and tacks that sometimes stick out of stuffed animals, pointed pieces of wood that have lost their rubber suction cups, and sharp edges of plastic and metal. Plastic wrappings and caps and guns that make too much noise can also create problems.

Most toys seem so harmless. But colorful rattles can break, and the bright balls inside might look good enough to eat. Chemical sets and toys for big children may get into small hands and rubbed into tired eyes.

Automobiles. Adult supervision is the best prevention, but so is quietly telling a child what to do and not to do, repeated again and again. Knowing "red" and "green" and looking both ways are still very important.

A car seat that is too big or too small, seat belts not used, and small children standing up in a moving automobile, or with arms or head outside the window, could mean trouble.

So can careless backing up in the driveway. It may lead to the scream of a hurt child, too small to be seen even if the rear view mirror is used.

A tricycle in traffic, a ball bouncing into the street, and thoughtless running between parked cars might all result in injury.

Medicines. "High up and hidden away" is the rule to follow. It's dangerous to say, "It tastes just like candy" because small children may then think it's all right to take a lot of it. Problems can be created by adult carelessness: Not reading labels; not emptying old bottles before putting them in the trash; giving medicine in the dark from the wrong bottle.

If you want to avoid danger for your young child, think about these too:

Playground equipment—sharp edges, bolts that stick out, and no adults to watch.

Sharp objects—pencils, tools, ice picks, scissors, knives, without a grown-up to show how to use them or what they are for.

Small objects—thumb tacks and marbles to swallow, and keys to put into open electrical wall outlets.

Tricycles—two or more riding at a time.

Household supplies—bleaches, garden spray, kerosene, insect powders, ammonia and moth balls not well enough hidden.

Stoves—with pot handles within easy reach.

Stairways without protective gates, *patio doors* without warning marks on the glass, *guns* that are loaded, *window screens* rusted or not fastened, *bath time* with no one to supervise, *old refrigerators* and *toy boxes* with large doors, *clothes lines* hanging too low—and the problems that *fire* and *water* can cause.

Just two more items for you to check: Do you have a first aid kit? Do you know how and when to use what's in it?

Perhaps most important of all is the way you act—for example, with tools, matches and other possibly dangerous items.

You want your child to be safe but not scared, careful but not timid, and have fun while playing, skating, swimming, and climbing a tree.

If you know the rules of accident prevention and safety, that's fine. A lot of parents do—but they sometimes need to be reminded.

15.

"Where Did I Come From, Mama?"
(A few words about sex and the young child)

This story has been told many times. It is about a young child who asked his mother, "Where did I come from?"

Thinking this was the moment for telling her youngster all about sex—how babies are started, the differences between boys and girls, and all the rest—the mother took a deep breath and jumped right in.

After a half hour of explaining (with drawings), she finally relaxed, and said, "Well, that's it, Johnny. Does that answer your question?"

In a puzzled way, little Johnny replied, "No, mama. You see, my friend Billy comes from Chicago, and I just wanted to know, where did I come from?"

So, RULE #1 connected with sex and the young child is this: *Answer the question he asks, and give only what he asks for—no more and no less.*

Some parents are surprised, and maybe even shocked, by what young children do, say and ask about sex.

If the baby discovers his fingers and toes, his happy mother and father are all smiles. But if he touches his sex parts, they may think it's "bad."

16.

Off to a Good Start in Arithmetic

Will your preschool youngster be good at arithmetic when he gets to school? Will he like it?

How he feels about it may depend on how you do. If it's hard or dull for you, it may be for him too.

But it doesn't have to be.

Some children get off to an unhappy start in arithmetic because they are forced to count and read or write numbers before counting and numbers really mean anything to them.

Try this: Place ten coins in front of your three or four year old child, and ask him to count them. Maybe he will point to the first one or two, and say the right numbers, but from then on he may be all wrong.

That's normal. He might be ready to begin learning about numbers although he can't always use them correctly.

You can help prepare him to use numbers later on by making *size, shape, direction* and *likenesses* and *differences* a part of your everyday conversations and not a special thing.

When you are with your young child as he or she is getting dressed, taking a bath, walking to nursery school, riding in a car, or going grocery shopping, you can start building toward numbers and counting. Both of you can enjoy it too.

Here are some easy beginnings:

SIZE—Using crayons, pencils, balls, silverware, dishes and members of the family, you can talk about and ask which is *largest, smallest, longest or shortest.* Make a game out of looking for the biggest and littlest articles in his room, in the back yard or on the playground. Help him see that there is *more* milk in this glass than in that cup, and *less* ice cream in the bowl after he has eaten part of it.

SHAPE—He can play with *squares, circles, triangles* and other designs that he sees in blocks or that you cut out of cardboard. You might get down on the floor and help fit them together. Shapes and designs are all around us—balloons, billboards, road signs—everywhere. You can help your child see them, but he is able to discover a lot about them by himself, too.

DIRECTION—Talk to him about pictures, leaves, flowers, birds and toys that are *above, below, inside, outside* or on something else. When you drive or turn to the *right* or *left,* you might sometimes tell him that you are.

LIKENESSES and DIFFERENCES—Help him put things together that belong together, like sorting out his socks, cans of food, buttons and pictures of animals. He will begin to see that some are the *same,* and others are *different.*

Point out other differences too—for example, in the *height* of children, the *speed* of automobiles and ants, the *weight* of rocks, cotton and sand, and the *cost* of candy and clothing.

Don't leave numbers out entirely, of course. Count with him when you clap hands, bounce a ball and set the table. Count with him as he points to objects in a row or as he goes up or down steps. Usually you can't go beyond five or ten with your preschool child, although he might be bright and able to do so.

Talk about *two* hands, *two* feet, *two* shoes and *two* eyes. The idea of *"five fingers,"* and a *"few* children," *"some* candy," *"many* people," and *"all* the toys" will come easily just a little later.

These ideas related to *size, shape, direction* and *likenesses* and *differences* should be kept simple. Although one well-known man said that any subject (including arithmetic) can be taught to anybody at any age, you and your youngster will enjoy it more if you take it easy, without pushing too hard.

Try not to be too serious about all of this. Your preschool child will learn most about the early stages of arithmetic as he experiments with blocks, toys and dolls, alone and with his friends.

You can get other ideas about the beginnings of numbers, counting and arithmetic from (1) your youngster's preschool teacher, (2) a good toy store with inexpensive toys based on sizes, shapes and patterns, and (3) the best children's television shows.

17.

"Don't Be Afraid, Little Boy/Girl"
(The fears of young children)

Young children can be afraid of many things:

Dogs and cats, and some large and little animals that don't even exist.

Dark places and loud noises, voices and laughter.

Doctors and dentists.

Vacuum cleaners, toilets, fire and water.

Others you can add.

Most of the fears of young children are normal and nothing to worry about.

They are serious only if they last too long or are too big for the small things that seem to cause them. If a little child is afraid of *all* animals or cries every time he or she goes to a preschool, to the bathroom or has a baby sitter, then perhaps you have a problem.

Most children's fears are based on what a child has seen or felt, but some he just imagines.

He is small, so large things may scare him. A slippery tub, his face under water, soap in his eyes, or huge waves might make him afraid of water. A noise he doesn't understand—like thunder—can bring tears. Being alone in the dark, even in his own room, may cause nightmares.

A wise parent knows how real all of this is to a small child. So you have two goals:

1. Prevent fears from becoming a habit.
2. Help your youngster be careful but not scared.

Here are a few examples of how they can be reached:

• Loud noises. Say, "Sometimes I still feel funny when it thunders even though I know it won't hurt me. When I was your age I was scared too."

• Darkness. "I'll stay with you for a while if you want me to. Yes, you can have a small night light if you'd like to have one."

• A large animal. "Some big dogs jump on people. Let's go up to this one together. We can ask his owner about him."

• Going down a slide. "You and I can watch the other children for a while. Then you can decide whether you want to go down."

Holding a child's hands and hugging him are important. Give him the feeling that (1) there is nothing to be ashamed of if he is scared, (2) many children and even some adults feel the same way and (3) "I'm here and I love you."

To tease a child or laugh at him because he is afraid could make him hide his fears, but they may then be buried deep inside and that's not good. It is just as foolish to tell him to be "brave," "big" or "strong" when he doesn't feel that way, or to threaten him with dark closets or scary people.

Discussing openly what he is afraid of is the best approach. Let him tell you, as many times as he wants to, how it felt to fall down, hear the fire siren close by, or be by himself when the lights went out. It often helps to talk things out, just as it does for grownups.

Some fears can be planned for, and avoided. If you'll be away for a while, talk about it ahead of time. If tonsils are to come out, explain what will happen in words he can understand. If there will be a new baby, recognize that he may be worried about someone taking his place. And if bedtime is preceded by a story, a song or a quiet game, nighttime fears may not occur.

A child who is frightened once shouldn't be exposed to the same scare soon again. You can't throw him into deep water, and expect him to laugh the next time you try it!

One who isn't ready to jump off a wall or fence shouldn't have to jump. If he does, he may be even more scared the next time.

When he understands something he might more easily accept it. Let him push the little switch that turns on the vacuum cleaner—and be there to smile and hold him.

Your own calmness, willingness to listen and explain, and patience even when the fears seem silly to you will help him overcome them. All fears and dangers can't be prevented, but you can make them less serious.

A happy child is one who can take them in stride.

18.

The Young, Gifted Child

Many parents are sure that their young children are bright—but it is so easy to be wrong.

Because they say clever things, put words together in unusual ways, and ask questions that may be hard for you to answer, you might think they are gifted. After all, if a child asks, "What makes the sky blue?" or "What makes thunder?" doesn't that mean he's very smart?

The problem parents face is that they often don't see their youngster in comparison with others. He or she may seem so quick—but others might be faster.

So here's a check list which can help you tell whether your preschool child is gifted. It is not necessary to score high on all twenty points, but if your youngster is strong on at least half of them, you can be quite sure he or she is bright.

Is your child gifted?

1. Started to walk and talk before most other children you know about.

2. Is at least a little taller, heavier and stronger than others his or her age.

3. Shows an interest in time—clocks, calendars, yesterday and tomorrow, and days of the week.

4. Learned to read even though not yet five years old. Likes to read.

5. Arranges toys and other possessions, putting the same kinds of things together.

6. Knows which numbers are larger than others.

7. Can count, and point to each item as he or she correctly says the number.

8. Creates make-believe playmates as he or she "plays house" or different games.

9. Is interested in what is on television and in newspapers, in addition to cartoons and comics.

10. Learns easily, so that you have to tell him or her something only once.

11. Shows impatience with jobs around the house that seem to have no meaning—like putting toys away when he or she is just going to have to take them out again.

12. Asks "Why?" often, and really wants to know the answer. Is curious about a lot of things, from a tiny insect and how it's "made," to a car and how it works.

13. Doesn't like to wait for other children to catch up.

14. Sticks with a task longer than others do. Won't give up easily.

15. Does things differently in ways that make good sense, whether it's piling up blocks, setting the table, or drying dishes.

16. Likes to be with older children, and can keep up with them.

17. Collects things, likes to organize them, and doesn't want anyone to mess them up—but doesn't always collect neatly.

18. Can carry on a conversation, and enjoys it. Wants your ideas and likes you to listen to his or hers. Uses big words and knows what they mean.

19. Shows an interest in drawing and music, knows

colors, and has rhythm.

20. Makes up jokes. Has a good sense of humor.

What should you do about it?

How does your preschool youngster come out on that list? Strong enough so that you feel he or she is gifted? All right—then are you ready for the next step?

Before going on, try to make up your own list of what to do. Write it on another sheet of paper. Cover up the rest of this page until you do.

Did your list include these? (1) Talk to him about what he does, likes and thinks; (2) listen to him; (3) read to him; (4) take him places; (5) enroll him in the best preschool, nursery school or day care center you can find and afford. And when he goes to school try to find the most creative, brightest teachers for him.

Your list, and mine, may make you think about something kind of interesting: These are, of course, the same things that parents should do for *all* of their young children.

74

19.

Kindergarten Comes Next

Is your young child going to kindergarten next fall? What can you do to help him or her get ready?

All kindergartens are of course not the same. There are three main types:

(1) One is like other grades in some schools where the teachers teach reading, arithmetic, science and all the rest, and want order and quiet.

(2) Another kind is much less "school-like." The children may not learn very much, but they might have a good time playing.

(3) Most are somewhere between those two. Work and play melt together in days filled with activities.

A good kindergarten is a busy, happy place. It is probably a lot different today than it was when you were five years old.

There are books and animals. Children plan and work, alone and with others. They make and read charts of colors, numbers, weather and room helpers. They use clocks and calendars. They learn safety with tools and equipment, and health habits in washing hands, using the toilet and sometimes eating meals. They learn to share ideas, finish tasks, and listen and follow directions. They get ready to read and use numbers.

All kindergarten teachers do not expect the same

things of the children who come to them. It is, of course, fine if your preschool child can tell time, knows the days of the week and months of the year (in order), and can make change and knows the names of coins. But all of that isn't always expected. There is time to learn such skills, plus the beginnings of reading as well as a home address and telephone number and how to write them.

A child who likes to be the center of attention and wants his or her own way may have a hard time adjusting to school. The one who is timid and says, "I can't," needs your help and patience to get over such feelings. The child who cries because her fancy dress or his new shirt or tie gets a little crushed or dirty needs to have you know how children should dress for their school day (in bright, durable, easily laundered clothing).

You can also do many other things to help your youngster prepare for kindergarten. Some of the main ones are *enough sleep* (about 10-12 hours each night), *balanced meals, a medical checkup* and necessary *shots*, how to use a *drinking fountain, toilet* away from home, and *handkerchief* (or *tissues*) correctly, and how to *cross streets*.

The dangers of wooden swings and throwing things are among the safety factors your child should know. The example you set for good health and safety is very important.

Go with him to visit the school and its playground. Talk about it as a happy place. Remember that it probably will seem very large, crowded and noisy to him. Expect him to be a little worried—but help him see it as a place of excitement and fun. Keep in mind that work is enjoyable for most young children, and school will probably be too.

Make an appointment to visit the kindergarten with

your child so that you both can find out about its program.

What did you each see there? Talk to him about it. Let him tell you what he liked and what he may have wondered about.

The activities you can provide will help make the move from home and preschool to kindergarten more smooth.

Read to him, let him tell or finish stories and button and zip himself up, visit the library with him, work out with him the household tasks he can do with dishes, clothes, putting toys away, caring for animals and watering plants.

Don't worry if he has been going to a fine preschool, day care center or nursery school and you think the regular school will not be as good. Whether he is 3, 5, or 15, *your plan should be to get the best education possible at all times.*

With kindergarten coming up soon, you can help most by (1) finding out and letting him find out what it will be like and (2) providing experiences and information that will make this new learning situation comfortable and happy.

20.

Television
Good or Bad for Young Children?

"Television viewing for the child under five should be wisely selected, seen by child and parent, and followed by a short fun discussion of what they saw."
Miss Frances
Ding Dong School

You should be involved right from the beginning with your young child in his or her television watching, says this expert.

Ask yourself how often you look at a program all the way through with your youngster. How often do you talk about one with him or her?

In many homes television fits into a different kind of pattern. The set is sometimes turned on early in the day and kept on whether anyone is watching or not. Or, there may be two sets on at the same time in different parts of the house.

Television isn't bad. The main problem is that it is often used badly.

In some families it is a young child's only activity. Some parents like it because it may keep children out of mischief and there is no mess to pick up or to trip over, no toys, clay, water, blocks or beads.

For both learning and entertainment, do you know

of anything else that costs so little and is always there ready for use? But just as it is with other parts of our lives—the family automobile, movies and meals, for example—television has to be planned for and used well.

Here are some suggestions for you to think about:

1. *Help choose the programs your preschool child watches.* It takes a little time. You have to watch them yourself once in a while.

2. *Select ones that are fun as well as those from which he or she can learn.* Some, of course, can both entertain and teach. You don't watch only educational adult programs; do you? You enjoy the ones you see, and so should your youngster. "The days that make us happy make us wise," said another expert in this field, and he meant that we, and our young children, can learn best if what we watch or do is also enjoyable.

3. *Talk about the program with your children, both before and after.* "What was it about?" "Why did the people do certain things?" "Which persons did you like—or dislike?" Keep your discussion short. A few minutes are enough. Let it be fun for both of you.

4. *Limit their TV watching.* That suggestion means nothing unless the other hours are enjoyable too. A good preschool, day care center or nursery school should be among your other first choices. Play with neighbors' children and sharing a little of your time are possibilities, too.

The problem with TV isn't so much what it does, but what it might prevent, like conversation, games, play with toys—and time with you. The television story may be good, but not as good as the one you make up with your child as the main character.

5. *Control your own television viewing.* The young child's main teacher is his or her parents. If you turn on the set the minute you get home and leave it on through

the late, late show, what can you expect? But if you select the programs you want and have a little peace and quiet around the house the rest of the time, your example can be a good one to follow.

Cartoons can be either good or bad. Popeye and his spinach still provide a useful bit of advice, and squashed insects and other animals come right back to life.

Violence on TV is something for you to watch out for. One study of nursery school children said that they imitated what they saw. Fighting, killing, and torture can wait until your young child is old enough to take them in stride. Middle-of-the-night tears and screaming can sometimes be traced directly to TV programs that are not suitable.

Watching television together can be boring unless you both enjoy it. Laughing at it, side by side, can be great. Try it out on this afternoon's or early evening's cartoons as a starter. Also do it on parts of "The Wizard of Oz" the next time it is shown.

So, in summary: *Select, control* and *use* television with your young child. It has a lot to offer.

21.

Your Young Child's Playmates
Friends or Enemies?

- Playmates are fun and important to have.
- They learn from each other, and get new ideas and language.
- Playing alone is sometimes important too.

Babies are not born with the ability to get along with others. In the early months they seldom even notice another infant. After a year or two they may show their feelings very plainly, by pushing, biting, pulling hair, or grabbing toys. They may play side by side, but not together.

The three-year-old might be ready for closer play, perhaps even for help in a block building, housekeeping or other project. At four or five, playing together is more common. All children are not ready at the same age to be with others, however.

One of the main changes in the preschool years is the increasing ability to be at ease with other children and adults. But the growth isn't smooth. Calm talking, playing and working together may take place, of course, but you can still expect some hitting, kicking and tears.

After all, even grown-up friendships don't always go smoothly. We've just learned to act better toward others than young children sometimes do.

Children often copy what they see in their own families. Those who are part of families that get along well together and respect the possessions and privacy of others are likely to be that way toward their playmates. Taking turns (if waiting isn't too long) can be learned at home in connection with which TV show to watch or who rides in the front seat of the family car.

You can help your young children get along well with their playmates in many ways:

• Teach them skills, like throwing a ball, riding a tricycle, or using clay and paints. Don't expect them to be very good with them, but they will then be more able to keep up with others.

• Take them places, like to the zoo and to see a bulldozer or crane. Let them help you around the house or on small repair jobs. Then they will be more fun for others to play with.

• Understand that children often want the same toy or wagon at exactly the same time. When it's not used, no one wants it. Such imitating is very common.

• Welcome your child's playmates. Be pleasant but firm with the frequent doorbell ringer and lunch visitor. Don't yell at or embarrass your children in front of their friends.

• Realize that a child who bullies others is usually unhappy. Showing kindness and an interest in him or her, or seeking and correcting the reason for the unhappiness, is important.

• Get them together with one child at a time and for short periods in the early years. Don't assume they will always like to be with the children of your friends.

• Seek playmates next door or at a nearby park or playground. Young children sometimes need help in finding other small children. Brothers and sisters are fine to have around, but they are not enough.

• Recognize that the best source of friendships (and the professional supervision to go with it) is a well-planned preschool, day care center or nursery school.

Parents sometimes don't understand that young children may make friends slowly. Looking at each other, quietly watching, and even playing alone while others are around are all part of the process.

Learning to cooperate takes time, but it doesn't mean that a child should meekly give in. When it's *my* turn, *my* toy or *my* stuffed animal, even a young child should be encouraged to stand up for his or her rights. That's not the same as being ready to fight.

Certain play materials and equipment help cooperation (wagons and tricycles, for example). Others are good for playing alone, like simple puzzles, paper and crayons.

Sometimes a child who had been friendly with others suddenly becomes shy. Perhaps it's because of a new baby in the family; or you've been away, and there is worry that you will be "taken away" again; or you have all moved into a new neighborhood; or there's a separation or divorce; or he or she has a health, hearing or sight problem. Talking it over and putting the problem into words, or correcting the health condition, may help turn on the earlier friendliness.

Your goal is quite clear: *A child at ease with others as well as by himself or herself is generally happy and well-adjusted.*

22.

Independence
Your Child Needs It

"Do it my own self . . . Let me do it . . . Yes, I can . . . Don't hold me so tight."

The second a baby is born he or she starts to become an independent person. But it isn't easy.

Parents want to hold tightly—and also let go. They may be sorry to see their children grow up, although they often are pleased when they learn to walk, get good school grades, or enter a profession later on.

Children want to be free—and still have their parents to depend on. For preschoolers that is especially true when they are tired, sick or lonely.

If you had to pick the major task of parenthood it might be this: *Help your child become independent and secure. Do it gradually. Be pleased when he or she can make decisions without your help.*

Years ago there was a play called "The Silver Cord." It was about a mother who controlled and finally destroyed her child.

There will always be a place for your suggestions and love, but the "silver cord" has to be loosened and cut. If it isn't, your child might never become an adult able to handle the problems of health, money, getting along with others, and so many more that we all face.

The preschool years are very important for starting your youngster toward independence. It can begin in your own home: *Dressing* without help (except at first, of course) . . . *playing* outside without supervision all the time . . . *picking up and putting away* toys, clothing and groceries . . . *taking* messages and running simple errands.

There are many other things you can do in these early years. Let him or her be away from you once in a while, at a good preschool or at a neighbor's house. . . . Hold back when you want to help solve a puzzle or problem. Let him do it his "own self." . . . Demand fewer kisses and hugs when the young child goes through a stage of not wanting them. . . . Accept the fact that a young friend may sometimes be wanted more than you are.

How much freedom you give depends on your own background, as well as on your children's desire and ability to do things on their own. They aren't all ready for preschool or staying overnight at a friend's house at the same age, for example.

A child's reason for doing things may sometimes be even better than yours. You may have difficulty saying yes when he wants to stay up a little longer (there may be interesting company in the house), watch the end of a TV show (it may be the best part), or not finish a meal (after all, our tastes for food sometimes differ).

If you are rigid, live by strict rules, and insist that he also should, your youngster may be afraid to try something new on his own.

Young children need practice and guidance. Instead of having a choice of whether to eat breakfast, they might be permitted to choose this cereal or that one . . . or this dress or that one rather than a choice from the whole closet. Parents still have to make some decisions for them, of course, like which shoes to wear in the rain and which clothing in the snow.

Children slide back once in a while, as when a new baby comes. The road to independence may have a few bumps in it. Dressing, eating and bathroom habits, for example, might suddenly seem to go backwards. "Let me help you *this* time" is then more sensible for you to say than "Aren't you ashamed?" or "You're old enough to know better!"

They like to do things well, but they need:

• *Success* with loose clothing, large zippers that work, a foot stool or box to help them reach the sink, low clothing hooks, attractive and tasty food, and simple household chores.

• Your *nice words and smiles* when they do tasks well *for their age.*

• Your *willingness to let them try,* try again, make mistakes, and then succeed.

All of that can lead to a child who feels good about what he or she does, gradually can do more and more on his or her own, and finally doesn't require a parent's help.

We may not like our children to need us so little—but isn't that really the main goal of most thoughtful parents?

23.

Reading with Your Young Child

Do you read to your young child?

Some parents start when a child is two. Some begin even earlier. Others never do because they feel they don't have time or it isn't important.

If you want your youngster to become a reader, to enjoy books, and to learn from them, you should begin reading to him or her early.

It will take only a few minutes each day, and it can help lead to a love for reading and toward a nice feeling for school and learning later on.

Reading with a young child can be enjoyable for you too. If you choose a story that is fun and a book with bright pictures, both of you can have a good time.

The list of books which youngsters like gets longer every year. You may be surprised at the many topics they cover and their colorful drawings and photographs.

Almost any young child can become excited by *fairy tales* and stories about *animals, other children, airplanes,* and *trains*. They can help open up a big, new world.

Here is a simple check list you can use to help start this enjoyable activity.

- Select books he will like. Get suggestions from a preschool teacher, children's librarian, or bookstore. These books don't have to cost much money, and those that he gets from the library with his own library card will probably cost nothing.
- Set up a daily schedule—like before bedtime or nap-time, or after dinner. Be ready to change it sometimes, for more important things such as being with a friend or having a snack.
- Notice if he or she gets bored, tired or cranky. Next time try to stop before that happens. *Reading to children should always be a happy experience for both parent and child.*
- Laugh together, wonder what will happen next, feel sorry if the child or animal in the story has a problem, and share a joyful ending when everything turns out all right.
- Read only part of a story once in a while, and let your youngster finish telling it. Ask, "What do you think happened next?" or "What should the boy (or girl) do now?" Then finish reading it so the endings can be compared.
- Read clearly and slowly. Show you enjoy the story.
- Let older brothers and sisters help out. They may like to share your reading to a younger child.
- Use the pictures. Ask, "What is happening here?"
- Let your youngster ask questions, and try to answer them. Talk about the story after you are finished.
- Tell old familiar stories about *The Three Bears*, *Little Red Riding Hood* and others, and then read them. The best ones are worth re-telling and re-reading many times.
- Help your child start to build his own library. Let

him put his name in his books (with your assistance if necessary).

• Subscribe to one or more children's magazines, ordering them in his name.

• Permit him to have quiet, free time to look at books all by himself.

• Use them to find out things. This can start the habit of looking up information.

• Buy books as presents sometimes, for your child and for others. Let him select them, unless they are to be a surprise for him.

Reading with young children isn't limited to books. There are (1) traffic signs like "Walk," "School Zone," and "Keep Right," (2) labels on food and signs in stores, and (3) TV commercials. Don't make a big thing out of reading all these with children. A little bit can go a long way.

Reading games can be fun too. Being the first to see a motel sign or a favorite hamburger billboard can be part of the reading process.

Just as important as the reading you do with a young child is the example you set. Your reading and how much you enjoy it can help set the stage for his or hers.

They learn by seeing you read from left to right, top to bottom, and front to back, and turn pages and use a proper light. But much more important is *the fun of it now and the later values toward which these few minutes a day can lead.*

94

24.

The Wonderful World of Toys

Toys are very important in the lives of young children. Books, games, and television may take their place as a child grows up. But during the preschool years he or she needs to play with toys.

Too often parents make mistakes in choosing them. They select toys (1) that *they* like rather than the toys a young child can enjoy, (2) that are too big or small, too advanced or babyish, (3) that don't do anything, (4) with which a youngster can't have fun, or (5) that are educational, but that's all.

A good starting point in selecting toys is to ask, "*What can he or she do with it?*" and "*How safe is it?*" Also worth asking are the questions, "*Will he or she like it?*" and "*What does it teach?*"

Some parents give too many toys to their children. (Have you ever seen a three-year-old on Christmas morning with so many that he didn't know which one to play with?) Just as serious is the problem of too few. Parents may not know how important toys are or they may feel that good ones are too expensive.

For young children, toys need not cost much, sometimes nothing at all. A box can become a wagon or a castle. Pieces of cloth can make a rag doll into a princess, and scraps of wood can be piled into a tower. A paper bag can seem like Daddy's lunch pail or brief case.

You provide the parts and a child brings the joy of imagination and discovery that makes them mean something to him.

Dr. Spock once said, "Children usually love the simple toys best, and play with them longest." He added, "The small boy pushing a block along a crack on the floor, pretending it's a train, is hard at work learning about the world."

Does your young child have the most *basic toys*—a ball, a doll (for boys too), a stuffed animal, and things with which to build, pretend (like a hand puppet), and draw (plus paper and a place to spread it out).

You might provide something for them to make music with too, remembering that what creates music for little children may not do so for you—pots, pans, and spoons, for example! How much clay and water paints they use depends on the space you have and how well you can control or overlook the mess.

Then there are outside toys, to sit or climb on, through, or under, to play in (a sandbox or play house, for example), to ride on, and to pull, push and carry. Because they may be expensive, you might be glad to let your youngster's preschool provide them.

You should sometimes expect a young child (1) to get tired of playing with one toy after a short while, (2) to be awkward in putting things together or piling them up, and (3) to be slow or stubborn in sharing his or her favorites with other children. All of that is normal behavior during the early years.

If a toy is to be worthwhile, a child should be able to do something successfully with it—perhaps fit it together, or hug or talk to it.

He should be safe with it, of course. If you check it for sharp points, sharp edges, loudness and small parts (so easy to swallow or choke on) you might save tears or pain.

The age label on the box in which a toy comes may or may not tell you whether your child will enjoy and learn from it. After all, children have different likes and grow up at different rates.

There are at least 5,000 new ones each year to choose from, and probably about 150,000 on the market that are made in the United States. If you don't like what the toy teaches, don't buy it. Get something else instead.

Toys can never take the place of your attention and love, of course. But a young child needs them very much.

A little television that you watch with him, a few books that you read with him, and some simple toys that he plays with alone, side by side with other children, and sometimes with you, can all help him feel good about himself and get ready for the big complicated world he is entering.

25.

The Young, Hyperactive Child

Some parents think their young child is hyperactive when he or she is merely doing what comes naturally.

Two, three and four-year-olds are often hard to live with. It is "normal" *once in a while* for them to have tantrums, move quickly from one toy or game to another, or wake up in the middle of the night.

We should not call children "hyperactive" unless they *really* are, and not just showing behavior that is usual for their age and development.

Characteristics

Are they *more* restless, difficult to get along with, and disruptive than other children of the same age? Do they cry, squirm, or fight more than others? Do they act in strange ways that they can't explain and you don't understand? Do they show little control over themselves and never seem to listen—but between times may be so sweet and lovable?

Other children are sometimes excitable and seem uncontrollable—but not most of the time. Others are sometimes sleepless, nervous, disorganized, or moody—but not almost all day or every night.

Hyperactive children often look like others. Their physical examinations seldom show any major differences. They are not mentally retarded although due to their unusual behavior they may do less well than others in playing games, completing little household chores, or listening to you read a story. They are not "bad" because they want to be, but they often act in ways that most adults don't like or can't accept.

Causes

Experts don't always give exactly the same reason why a certain youngster is hyperactive. However, they usually agree that more boys are hyperactive than girls.

A child "acts out" because he or she has a neurological disease or disorder... or has had a childhood sickness or accident ... or lives with or apart from arguing, separated, unloving or uncaring parents ... or never receives praise ... or is hurt or rejected physically or emotionally.

Add to that list difficulties of mother or child before birth or injuries at birth and you have most of the reasons why a child may be hyperactive.

What to do about it

Hyperactivity is a symptom and not a cause. To eliminate or reduce it the cause should be identified (if possible), and minimized.

You may not be able to do it alone, needing assistance from a physician and a skilled nursery or day care teacher.

If your child is mildly hyperactive, preschool encouragement and supervised play may be helpful. If severely hyperactive, you shouldn't expect teachers to provide one-to-one help. You'll need the necessary combination of medical, psychological and psychiatric support. Your doctor may be the one with whom to start.

However, the first approach to the problem should begin even earlier, at home.

Among the specific things you can provide are these:

- A structured routine of dressing, meals, and cleanliness.
- His room kept in order, with your help.
- Tasks at which he can succeed, and rewards when he is successful.
- Consistent discipline that makes sense to him.
- Time you schedule alone with him.
- A substitute for mother or father if either one is missing.
- A record of your child's behavior; when, where and under what circumstances does the hyperactivity occur?

Drugs or other medication may be necessary, but only if (1) other means don't work and (2) a physician recommends them. Some possible side effects to drugs may develop, including being depressed or withdrawn. That's one of the reasons for research on other kinds of controls, like removing artificial food coloring and flavoring, reducing iron deficiencies and giving them coffee. Such research is still in process.

Most children outgrow hyperactivity to at least some extent by adolescence. However, it is sometimes easier on the family if drugs (under supervision) are used in the pre-adolescent years.

Whether a child is called "hyperactive," "hyperkinetic," or "minimal brain damaged," he or she needs your help, and the earlier the better. Otherwise, school failure or emotional disturbances may come. Some of these later difficulties might be avoided if you:

(1) recognize the problems that can lead to them while your child is young.

(2) provide the environment he needs, including plenty of both structure and love.

(3) seek outside professional assistance when necessary.

26.

Telling the Truth
It Isn't Easy!

"It's *my* toy!"

"Yes, I *did* wash my hands."

"I just took *two* cookies."

"There was this big man . . . and he came in my room when you put out the light . . . and he grabbed me . . . and . . ."

It isn't easy to tell the truth all the time, especially when you are two, three, four or five.

But when a young child does *not* tell the truth, is he or she lying on purpose? Or are there other reasons for the wrong words to come out?

"*My* toy" is often said because he or she wants it so much, even though it is really understood that it belongs to someone else. Little ones know that parents want to hear that their children are clean, so it's easier to say that they *did* wash their hands. Isn't that a lot better than explaining that the water was too hot, the faucet too tight, or the task done well would have meant being away too long from where all the fun was?

Mama may be angry if I took more than *two* cookies, so that's a good number to tell her. And it may be fun to imagine or to fool people about that big man in the dark. Besides, that story might help keep Mother or Dad in the dark room with me.

Telling the truth doesn't come naturally. It has to be learned, and that takes time. It is so easy not to tell the truth in order to *avoid punishment* ("No, I didn't cross the street"), *get parents' approval* ("Yes, I picked up all the toys"), *feel older* ("I can too go down that slide"), *escape blame* ("baby sister spilt the milk") or *create excitement* ("their house fell right down").

Because a child sometimes doesn't know all the right words to use, or hasn't yet learned differences in sizes, shapes or directions, he or she may stretch the truth—like "I saw lots and lots of fire engines" (although maybe there were only two) or "His daddy has the biggest car in the world."

Everyone needs recognition and affection, and children may lie for them. After all, what's so serious about saying that I did what you wanted and then you'll give me a smile or a kiss? It may also seem to be worth a little lie to see how surprised people look and to get a father who seldom visits to stay longer. A young child doesn't often think ahead to the fact that you may find out the truth.

Young children can't always tell the difference between "real" and "pretend," or between make believe for fun and telling a lie to get something they want.

So what can you do about it? Here are some practical hints:

• Recognize that lies are part of every young child's life.

• Try not to use the word "lie" or to call him a "liar" when you are not getting the whole truth. If he thinks you have a low opinion of him, his main reason to try better may be destroyed.

• Understand that he is less likely to lie again if he knows you aren't fooled, that you don't like it when he lies ("although I never stop loving you"), and that his lies upset his friends.

- Explain that "make believe" and "really true" aren't the same. Two is too early to try to explain, but by three or four it may be pretty easy.

- Say, "Tell me what you really saw (or took or did)" rather than "Don't you dare lie to me, young man." Severe punishment sometimes leads to their becoming more skillful at lying instead of being more truthful.

- Prevent situations that encourage lies. It doesn't help to ask whether hands were washed when you can see how dirty they still are. If you ask, you might have two problems, carelessness and lying. So don't ask; tell or take instead.

- Recognize that a child who *always* seems to lie or make believe may need professional help. But a little bit of it is completely normal.

- Set the example yourself. It's probably your own business when you boast about cheating in work or play or lie about your age, but do your young children have to hear you? If you can't avoid the original act, perhaps you can at least stop talking about it. Lying is kind of contagious, and young children learn from what they see adults do.

- Break promises or give dishonest answers, but recognize that's a form of lying too.

You Grow Up?"

early to think about
n? Is it too early to do
r girl growing up will
f course not.

portant to parents.
ought about. Parents
ill do when he or she
en the youngster is
l through something
nple, but how about

your young child's
you do about it?

ways to start out, to
s in school:

rk, what your job is,
rk a full day almost
d doesn't see you for
uring that time is a

• Give him just a little information at a time about what you do. Answer his questions in words he can understand.

107

• Ask his preschool teachers if they ever visit people at work or invite men and women in to talk about their jobs. Those who work on the local newspaper, at the zoo, or in the gasoline station are often ready to come in. They just have to be asked.

• Offer to go there and tell about your own job once in a while. Sit down on the floor or on a little chair and talk to the children. Five minutes may be long enough to tell them what you do and why you do it. Tell them the reasons honestly—because you like the work, or it brings in money, for example. After all, going to nursery school usually costs something, so you work to keep your child there as well as to buy food, clothing and a place to live. Or invite them to visit you on the job. Your child will be so proud of you!

For a long time schools have discussed with children the subject of "community helpers" (policemen, firemen, mailmen and a few others). Now we can do a lot more, and earlier.

Mothers and fathers have many kinds of jobs. In talking about them we can begin to give young children the idea that some women as well as men are doctors, lawyers and, yes, even cab and truck drivers. Some men are nurses, telephone operators and teachers of young children.

Through what children eat, wear and see we can also start giving them a picture of the world of work.

• How did the bananas, oranges and chocolate get into our kitchen?

• Who made your shoes, sweater and hat?

• How did that big billboard advertising new cars or homes get put up? Who builds those cars and homes anyway?

All of this may take a little homework on the part of parents, maybe with the help of a good preschool teacher, a nearby librarian or the encyclopedia.

This job talk with young children can easily be overdone, so please be careful. Don't buy toys only because they tie in with some occupation; trucks, nurse kits and play stoves should be fun to play with, not bought just because they relate to jobs.

You lose some important time in a child's early years if you act as though his future work will never come. It will, sooner than you now think, and helping him see that people do many, many things will begin to open his mind and eyes to what he might someday do himself.

One government agency puts out a book that lists more than 35,000 jobs. It's unfair to keep a child in the dark about all but the typical "community helpers," plus maybe his doctor and the grocery clerk.

If he or she hears at home and preschool at least a little bit about what people do to earn a living, the "career education" and school and job decisions that come later on will make more sense.

Many of us seldom thought about the job world until we were grown or almost grown. Our young children will perhaps enter it more smoothly if we once in a while share with them what we and others do on our jobs.

28.

Traveling with Your Young Children
Some Hints for Survival!

Have you ever traveled with young children? Did you know that sometimes it can really be fun?

There are two factors that can help you avoid tears, temper tantrums and tension:

• *Personality*—your own. If it is hard for you to be patient when your youngsters ask you for the tenth time, "Are we almost there?" (and you're barely out of the carport), you have these choices: leave them at home as much as possible, or keep reminding yourself that young children weren't meant to sit still, be quiet and act polite all the time.

• *Preparation.* Here's where you can show how smart you are. It can make all the difference in the travel with them being either miserable or a real pleasure.

Preschool children get restless, so they need *interesting things to do and a variety of items to play with.* They get tired, so they need *rest and occasional stops.*

Most travel with young children is by car, and that's fortunate. You can then control the schedule, and adjust meal, running-and-jumping and sleeping time.

Remember one important point: All children are different. What satisfies one child may be a complete bore to another. So try to answer this question carefully: What does this youngster like to do at home? His or her interests won't change the minute the car door shuts, so what was fun at home may also be enjoyable on your trip.

Here's a check list for your "travel survival kit":

- A place in the car that is his very own.
- A toy suitcase or bag of his own. In it can be coloring books, paper, blunt scissors, crayons, clay, small paper or plastic dolls and some doll clothing (for boys too), small cars and trains, cardboard and cutouts to fold and put together, new and familiar books he can look at and that you can read to him; also a favorite doll or stuffed animal for bedtime.
- Fruit, snacks, salted crackers (said to be helpful for car sickness), cheese, hard-boiled eggs in their shells, a thermos (with milk, fruit juice or water) and a bag for trash.
- A pillow and blanket.
- Clothing that doesn't show much dirt or need ironing.
- Cleansing and toilet tissues that you can get to quickly.
- Plastic table cloths for picnics and also for bed wetters—and maybe a toilet seat.

There are so many things to do in the car: Read to them. Sing together. Play games; take some and make up some, like "Who sees ... ?," based on colors, animals, trees, billboards or whatever magic in the outside world passes through the car window. Stop at playgrounds and parks once in a while too.

Be as careful as you can of the food they eat. Salad dressings, puddings and pastries with moist fillings may be spoiled. Try as much as possible to stay with hot foods, fruits you can peel, and the food you take along, rather than overdoing the snack routine.

An early morning start, regular mealtimes, naps and quiet time, stops (to uncage all of you during the day!) and a stop for the night by late afternoon can round things out—except for one important item:

Safety.

It can help make the trip safe if you lock the car doors and don't let the children stand on car seats. Perhaps it would be wise even to put a pad or blanket over the back of the front seat. Take a basic medicine kit, and let them run and play only where you can watch them.

Something to look forward to is so nice, whether it's ice cream, a picnic or a swimming pool. But ten minutes to a young child may seem as long to him or her as a twelve-hour wait for a cup of coffee might be for you!

The car won't always be orderly or serene, so don't expect it to be. Be prepared to "roll" with a little turmoil, but planning ahead can cut it down.

Preparation will also help for plane, train and bus travel. The hints here can be a good starting point in getting ready for it.

You're not the only one sometimes caught in what may seem like a noisy, cluttered human cage on wheels. You have lots of company.

Happy traveling!

29.

Changing the Behavior of Young Children
Can It Be Done?

Does your preschool child do some things you don't like? Does he or she hit or bite, refuse to eat or go to sleep, or fail to put toys away? Do you want to improve things and make life more pleasant for both of you?

You have two choices: continue as you are, perhaps with nagging, screaming, and hitting of your own, or go at it with a plan, in an orderly way. The first choice may seem easier, but it's probably not very successful. The second takes longer, but it may work better.

Some behavior is changed by time. Dressing himself, eating neatly and going to the bathroom are examples where maturity and the right models to copy may take care of the situation. But improving other kinds of behavior needs your active help.

You can start by asking, "What do I want to change? What behavior do I think needs improving?" Begin by making a list of what he or she does that bothers you.

There are two major parts of what you can do to encourage better behavior, whether it's related to whining, striking out at others, taking things or almost anything else that you feel is wrong.

• *Keep a record of what behaviors you see that you want to improve.*

Whenever you notice it, write it down. Do so for only one kind of behavior at first because it takes practice to keep notes of this kind. For example, how often does he or she cry for what seems like no reason? If you know the reason, like being over-tired or catching a cold, then removing the cause or relieving the illness may solve the problem.

However, even if you know of no reason, you can start toward getting rid of the tears.

● *Use affection and praise to work for good behavior. Try, if possible, to pay no attention to the kind of behavior you want to stop.*

At first the tears or misbehavior may come even more often, but stopping them requires your sticking with a detailed procedure. When parents continue to give in, to provide the attention a child strives for when he does what we don't like, he has no reason to stop.

You'll have to notice very small changes for the better and react to them right away. Your words, smile, hug or just the quiet attention you give (like to a shy child who makes even a slight effort to join another youngster) may be enough. Perhaps you can offer a small reward. "When you put your toys away and get ready for bed, I'll have a treat for you (milk and cookies)." Some people call this "bribery," but it isn't. Bribery is a reward for doing something wrong.

This approach is sometimes referred to as "Grandma's Law." "Do what I want and you'll get what you want" or "Work before play." That "play," or reward, should be something your child likes. We have to remember that what may be a chore for us isn't to pre-school youngsters. They like to help you wash the car and set the table, and to run errands or be carried on Daddy's shoulders.

Our habit of finding fault is often a trap. Yes, it

might get a child to pick up his clothes or wash his hands this time, but it may be only temporary. You may have to nag him every time you want something done.

Many studies indicate that if we use certain words, expressions and physical closeness they may help us improve children's behavior.

So try *words* like these when you see the smallest hint of improvement: "You did a good job," "Fine," "I'm so pleased" and "Let's tell your Dad." Or use certain *facial expressions* more often: smiling, laughing, looking interested, nodding approval. Or get *closer* by touching, hugging, sitting down on the side of his or her bed, or offering your comfortable lap.

If rewards are used to get small improvements started, they can be given less frequently as the tantrums or other troublesome activities occur less often. Finally, by the time the bad habits are over, you won't have to think about providing rewards.

Researchers have worked hard in this whole field of changing children's behavior. They use words like "behavior modification," "reinforcement," "extinction," "modeling " and "shaping."

Their goal is the same as ours: Increase the good behavior, reduce or eliminate the bad, and make our children's lives happier—and our own too.

118

30.

The Large Muscles in Little Children

Before a child goes to school he has to learn many important things. Among the most important are how his body works and how to use his arms and legs.

Although they all come together kind of naturally, you can help prepare for the large and small muscle development everyone needs.

Teachers and others talk about "gross motor" (large muscle) and "fine motor" (small muscle) activities. With a little time and some inexpensive equipment you can help your young child make good use of the controls and strengths important now and later.

He or she will of course run, jump, climb, hop and skip without your involvement, but you may not be aware of the large number of skills you can help add.

How much equipment and material are available in the preschool your child attends, or in your own yard or neighborhood playground or park? (No child needs all of it. All children can learn by using much of it, however.) And is it all *safe* and *sturdy*? It'll be taking a lot of punishment.

- Equipment and materials

Stairs
Barrel
Seesaw

Skates
Wheelbarrow
Balls (all sizes)
Boxes and blocks
Slide and bars
Swings and gym set
Shovel and broom
Tricycle and wagon
Boards (2 X 4 and
    flat ones)
Trains, trucks and cars
Ladder (rope and wall)
Bean bags and hoops

No two children (even in the same family) mature at the same rate or necessarily like the same playthings. Your child may enjoy some of those listed above; a different child might prefer others. Yours may be ready for some when he or she is three; others are ready earlier or later.

Here are a few sample activities the experts say that preschool children can often do at different ages. Remember, your youngster may be slower or faster and still completely "normal."

● 2-3 year-olds
Runs without falling
Opens doors; turns door knobs
Walks up and down stairs
Jumps with both feet
Builds small block tower
Stands on tiptoes
Tries to stand on one foot

● 3-4 year-olds
Rides a tricycle
Kicks a ball
Jumps from bottom step

Throws ball overhand
Walks on a circle without stepping off
Changes feet going upstairs or on a board (or "balance
  beam")
Stands and hops on one foot

- *4-5 year-olds*

Jumps while running or standing still
Stops, starts and turn corners quickly
Changes feet going downstairs
Builds tall block tower
Hops on one foot
Balances well on toes
Climbs ladders and trees
Walks heel to toe

One example of "equipment" that almost any child
can have is an old automobile tire. What he or she does
with it may surprise you—walking on the rim, jumping
in and out, and feet on the tire with hands on the floor.
With a few tires children often jump from inside one to
another, and run forward and backward in designs and
patterns that are fun for them.

Although a young child needs independence in
developing muscular coordination, balance and
strength, parents and teachers can be very helpful.
Showing how, doing with, holding hands, and *praising
effort and success* can all pay off. Start with what he or
she can now do and lead into new activities.

Does this all sound like a tough job for parents? It
certainly doesn't have to be, if you bring at least a little
time and patience to it. You may be surprised—you
might even enjoy it.

One thing is very sure—your young child certainly
will.

31.

The Only Child

Do you have an only child in your family?

Did you know that only children have often been identified as "different?" Back in 1898 some research said they were below average in health, subject to physical or mental problems, and peculiar.

A research study in 1927 agreed. It stated that these children are usually "jealous, selfish, egotistical, dependent, aggressive, domineering or quarrelsome." (That in itself is almost enough to encourage a second pregnancy or an adoption!)

Then came a study that disagreed with all of that. It stressed their self-confidence and leadership. Another one said these youngsters weren't different at all, although they did seem to be finicky in their food tastes and had temper tantrums more often than other children.

So what's the truth about only children?

Although there are of course numerous exceptions, these children *are* sometimes handicapped in their adjustment to others. They may be limited in their opportunities to play and compete with other children and sheltered from the normal give-and-take of childhood. They are more often caught in a bind simply because there are no other children for parents to watch, nag and love.

The importance of a good preschool program may therefore be pretty obvious to you.

If you are the parent of an only child, you may tend toward being overly protective, as often happens with the first born. This attitude could exist because only children are occasionally born to older parents or to those who want to but can't have any others.

So you may worry over small illnesses, praise them too much for doing little things, and interfere too often. A headache, a star on an ordinary school paper, and an invitation to another youngster's birthday party may become too big a thing.

The early involvement of many of these children with adults might lead to other children disliking them. After all, who wants to play with a child who uses big words and seems to think he's better than the rest?

Some of the problem times for only children are when they go to school for the first time (others also may cling to mother, but perhaps not as much), bedtime with too many books and records and maybe lying down with the youngster for too long, and mealtimes with coaxing and catering to food fads and whims. Such situations occur in other families, of course, but might take place more frequently when there's an only child.

These children often have a lot of advantages. There could be more money for education, toys and clothes when there is only one child to spend it on. Parents have more time for one than when it has to be shared with many, and there may also be more vacations and travel.

Because of such advantages they might seem brighter than other children, reflecting the time and enrichment given to them.

Most parents of only children know they could have a problem on their hands, and sometimes work hard to avoid it. Nursery school and summer camps if the family budget permits, having other youngsters come to visit as much as possible, and broadening their own interests and activities so the child becomes less of a center of attention are all good practices to consider. It's better for him if his parents get involved in their own music, art, or school or college courses, anything productive and unrelated to this youngster. The child will probably get plenty of attention anyway.

The possible difficulties are sometimes made worse by grandparents if they have only one grandchild. There could be similar problems if there's only one boy among a group of sisters, or just one girl among the boys. Any situation where pampering may occur requires being careful to keep the youngster from dominating the family.

An only child may be lonely and dependent, but he could just as well be the most popular child on the block. It all depends on the personality with which he was born and how well his parents balance their love and concern with an awareness that they can give and do too much.

Only children may be no more selfish or hard to get along with than children in larger families. They may be no brighter. Just like the oldest, youngest and handicapped, they are children first.

32.

Your Infant in a Day Care Program

If you and your husband (or wife) both have to—or want to—work, what should you do with the baby? If you're a single parent who works, what should you do with him or her during your working day?

Where can he or she be placed to assure good care and to reduce your guilt as close to zero as possible?

If you select wisely, there shouldn't be any guilt at all. In fact, babies of working parents can often profit from the added experiences an infant setting provides.

A neighbor or relative may be the easiest (and cheapest) solution. It's not necessarily the best one, however, not if you're lucky enough to find a day care center or extension of a preschool setting that prides itself on the human warmth, cleanliness and competence of its service and staff.

However, it takes more than luck and a hasty drop-off at the store right around the corner to select a high quality spot. On the surface it may seem to be first-rate, but what happens after you leave the baby there each morning?

No one needs to tell you that the responsibility is yours to check into the people and place in detail. But what should you look for?

The main things you have to check are items related to:

- who the people are who have contacts with your baby.
- what they do with him or her. Do they have a program?
- how clean, colorful and pleasant the total environment is.

First of all, visit the center and talk to its staff. Check on as many of the items below as you can. There are, of course, others that may be important to you and necessary to meet your baby's special needs, but these are a start anyway.

If they resent, are uncomfortable about or refuse your request to visit, you may have received the first warning. Perhaps they have nothing at all to hide, but then why are they reluctant to have you go in? Does their explanation make sense to you?

Here's a check list that you can use. The more "Yes" answers you give the more comfortable you can feel about leaving your infant there. But even one "No" can be serious unless there is a logical substitute or reason.

- Do staff members appear warm and affectionate? Do they look at the infants, smile at them and show them different facial expressions?
- Are the babies given individual attention and frequently held?
- Do staff members do some or all of the following: Talk to infants; sing to them; play records in their room; point out objects of special interest, like "Here is your bottle."
- Is an adult always in the room with the infants?
- Are there arrangements for bathing infants when necessary—and are they safe ones?

- Is smoking prohibited in the room where the babies are?
- Are toys free from sharp edges, parts that can fall off, be bitten off or swallowed, lead chips, and potential electric shock?
- Is the equipment in good shape?
- Are the floors clean, with a non-skid or carpeted covering?
- Is a Department of Health license on display or available?
- Does the center allow (or even encourage) parents to visit at any time during the day?
- Are colorful pictures and other decorations displayed in the room?
- Are some of these toys available: Rattles; rubber and cuddly dolls and animals; form and nested boxes; puzzles with large, simple, brightly colored pieces.
- Does the room appear uncrowded?
- Are there no more than three infants in an area the size of a normal bedroom (about ten by twelve feet)?
- Are some pull, push, and pounding toys available?
- Are infants taken out of their cribs or playpens?
- Does the center have a sand box and sand toys for the older infants?
- Do staff members offer them squeeze and small stacking toys, and permit them to "finger feed" themselves?
- Is play dough available for the older infants?
- Are there mirrors in the room?
- Is the sound level low and controlled?

Perhaps the most important question of all is this one: "Do I get the feeling, the over-all impression, that these people will take good care of my baby?"

33.

Do Young Children Worry?
(Moving away, getting hurt
or a death in the family)

It isn't possible to shelter children from all pain and sorrow. A king once tried. He wanted the young prince's life to be so perfect that he would never face danger, fear or death. He even had the royal gardeners snip off fading flowers every night while the little prince slept. But in the end even he found out about sadness and trouble, as we all must.

Young children can face problems more easily when their parents and preschool teachers use clear and honest words, smiles and hugs to ease them through difficult times.

The fears of young children can be very real to them. Darkness, loud noises, animals, doctors—the list is long. However, there are ways to prevent them from becoming a habit and to help your youngster be careful without being scared.

One of the most difficult problems for parents are those related to a broken family and how they affect a young child. Mother, father and home are his or her whole world. But neither divorce nor separation will necessarily destroy it.

Little children sometimes worry about matters other than separated or divorced parents and everyday fears like being alone in the dark or getting soap in his or her eyes.

- *Moving to a new place*

The problem of leaving somewhere that is familiar can be planned for in advance and handled when it happens. The important thing to remember is that most children (and adults too) feel better when their own belongings are around them. Having their own toys, books and other playthings can reduce feelings of loneliness. Most important, of course, is being with their own family, if possible, no matter where they live.

Even small children can understand they have to move if the reason is explained in simple words. "Daddy will look for a job there" or "We will have more money to buy food and other things we need" are ideas that are usually easy to accept.

When parents can adjust to new situations, it is easier for the children to take them in stride. Adult arguments and tears over leaving friends and family too often rub off on the youngsters. You can't (and shouldn't) hide your deep worries about the change, but neither should you let yourself expose them too openly. That's just too much of a burden for a young child to carry.

- *Getting hurt*

When a little child sees a handicapped person, he may think (or say), "Can that happen to me?" At the top of a slide, he might tell you, "No! I'll fall down!" When a little girl becomes aware that she's "made differently" from boys, she may wonder, "What's wrong with me?"

Childhood worries like these require honesty and openness.

What you say, like "You won't be hurt," "I'll help you," "Let me hold your hand," and "I'll stay here and watch," will show that your youngster can depend on you. "Boys and girls *are* made differently" can help put to rest the idea that something is wrong, missing, or hurt.

- *A death in the family*

What you say about it to a young child is important. *How* you say it may be even more important. Whispers and secrecy can be a mistake.

A young child usually doesn't ask for or need a lot of details. "Why do people die?" (Your answer might refer to "old," "weak," or "his (or her) body wore out.") "Will I die too?" (Everybody does some day, but it will be a long, long time from now.) "What happens to them then?" (Your answer will, of course, depend on your religion. The most honest answer for many of us is, "We don't really know." Telling a young child that "they go to sleep" can be dangerous, possibly creating bedtime fears.)

Keeping him or her on a regular schedule, with meal, preschool, TV and other activities moving along as normally as possible can be helpful when there's a death in the family. If you release your own feelings to a limited extent, a child will be more free about showing his or hers. Feelings are easier to talk about when they are in the open.

It's also wise to recognize that if boys show concern and sometimes cry they are taking an important step toward becoming men who are sensitive to the feelings of others, including those of their own wives and children.

34.

Are You a Working Mother?

* "I'm working and have very little time to spend with my children. After all, when I get home, there's dinner to make, and washing, ironing and cleaning to do."

* "How much am I hurting my children by going to work?"

You may not be hurting them at all. In fact, taking a job might be the best thing you can do for them. Enjoying your work, making extra money, and feeling good about yourself are all important factors for the working mother to consider. Two jobs in the family often make the difference between skimpy and satisfying meals, not having or having at least a short summer vacation, and TV dinners and TV watching at night instead of eating out once in a while and an occasional night on the town.

For single mothers the job may be even more necessary than when there is another pay check coming in.

But for them, too, the nagging question may keep coming up: "What am I doing to my young children by being away so much?"

Most working mothers should feel no guilt at all about taking jobs, according to some of the research on this subject. In fact, it often indicates that many mothers who either have to or want to work should obtain both pride and pleasure from the fact that they can do two jobs well, one at home and the other outside.

Dr. Lois Wladis Hoffman of the University of Michigan found that—

- When mothers like their jobs, their attitudes rub off on their children. They help make their home a happier place.

- Daughters of working mothers have a more modern, open view of women's place in the world than the one of girls whose mothers are limited to a housework/bridge/cooking routine.

- Working away from home doesn't seem to deprive school-age children of much, if anything.

- Many working mothers tend to have a false picture of the non-working mother-child relationship. The at-home mother may not use her time to read to children, play games with them and take them places as much as the one who works may imagine.

Just because you are employed doesn't necessarily mean you will spend less time with your youngsters. Your good sense or guilt feelings, or both, may encourage you to use the early morning, evening and weekend hours more carefully and waste them less than a mother who is there all the time.

Planned activities, a Saturday afternoon movie together, before-bedtime reading, enjoying togetherness in watching a TV program—these may be a regular part of your schedule. You are more likely to plan your time carefully and guard closely the limited number of hours you have at home.

However, you also have to guard against too many presents and treats, like candy and ice cream, just because you have a job and less time for your youngsters.

Whether you work or not isn't the key point in the development of your children anyway. Far more important are items that may not be related to your job situation at all.

A check list like this one indicates matters of more importance in your child's growth and adjustment:

• Do parents get along well with each other?

• Do they like what they do with most of their waking hours, whether inside or out of the home?

• If only one lives in the home, is he or she adjusted to single "blessedness"?

• Is some time scheduled with each child alone, the amount of it related to the youngster's needs?

• Are the common sense attitudes of non-favoritism, discipline, and love (shown through words, touching, holding, and kissing) used with all?

• Do your young children attend a preschool whose personnel and program you have checked into thoroughly?

Going to work or not isn't the major factor in the relationships we have with our children. How we feel about our lives and theirs, and how we show such feelings are more vital.

Although we started out talking about working mothers, most of what's been said also applies to their fathers, of course.

35.

Boys and Girls . . . and What to Expect

• *Little boys* playing house and with dolls, crying, showing their concern and feelings toward others . . .

• *Little girls* climbing trees, hammering, playing baseball, putting together mechanical things . . .

When parents worry about young boys doing "feminine" things and preschool-age girls interested in "boyish" activities, they may be behind the times. Numerous activities of ours that are recognized as male and female by many people overlap these days.

Look at Little League and tennis, long hair and colorful clothing, fathers in hospital delivery rooms, in the kitchen and changing babies' diapers, and mothers earning a living, repairing the car and balancing the monthly bank statements.

How you feel about the activities of your own young children, what you say to them about their "male" and "female" involvements, and what example you set depend on (1) how you were brought up yourself and (2) how much you recognize the changes taking place all around us.

When many of us were young, boys were boys and parents usually felt that they had to be tough, protective and sports-minded. Girls were expected to be feminine

139

and dependent. Some of those expectations still exist, of course. Every society has certain male and female roles related to work and family, but the line between them is less clear these days.

Do you really believe that all men are better with tools and have to "take it" without tears even when it hurts? Do only women change their minds and become poor automobile drivers?

Male and female behavior begins in early childhood. It depends on what parents and teachers of young children think is important. A little boy who helps his father fix a faucet and receives a smile as a "thank you" begins to get the idea that approval comes from such activities. The little girl who helps mother make a cake and receives a hug in return knows that it pays off to do "female" things.

Young children copy their parents without even knowing they do. Watch how your children walk, eat and act toward others, and you'll see a little (or a lot) of yourself. Listen to them talk to other children, and you'll quickly see how much you influence their behavior by your example. The copying by small boys of their fathers and girls of their mothers is so clear.

Here are some factors related to the attitudes of boys and girls toward the sex that they are:

• A father can be gentle, not necessarily a "sports nut," and still provide a strong example for a boy to follow. More important is the fact that he makes decisions, carries family responsibilities and is admired for the many things he does.

• A mother can work and share the family burdens, but still show her young daughter the satisfaction she derives from being a woman.

• Parents are often attracted to their own

youngsters of the opposite sex. For example, it isn't unusual for the feminine little girl to be difficult all day (with her mother) and a complete pleasure in the evening (with her father).

• Just because you are a "single parent family" doesn't mean your son or daughter will necessarily lose a great deal because the "proper" model isn't there.

• Attitudes toward their own sex and body and toward the opposite sex begin early. You can help form them in a healthy way.

• Young children sometimes compete for the affection of the opposite parent—boys against fathers, girls against mothers. It is usually a losing battle and doesn't last long.

It's not fair to young children to try forcing them to be only hard or callous without affection or tenderness (boys) or to assist and watch without being involved (girls).

The example we set and what we expect can help them grow up to realize that:

(1) both sexes are important.

(2) many things that interest one sex can also interest the other.

(3) to be "the man of the family" or "the woman of the house" may not really differ much in connection with the many things they both do and enjoy.

36.

Money . . . Money . . . Money

Many of us spend more time earning money and deciding how to use it than we do on anything else. However, few of us think about it much in connection with our young children.

But we should, from two points of view—ours and theirs.

Our income has to take care of all the everyday family needs, of course. Food, health, clothing and home expenses must be covered, but then what? Vacations and travel? Insurance? Movies and restaurants?

No matter what other uses for money are important to you, the cost of your preschool child's basic start in life should be high on your list.

A good early childhood education program can pay off in many ways. For example, few parents can supply the professional supervision available in a well-developed preschool. Nor can they usually provide broad communication, behavior, physical, number and pre-reading skills—or safe, large, and varied equipment and materials.

You certainly may do a great deal at home, but a sound preschool can expand your young child's environment and help him or her to do well when the later school program starts.

So when you decide on how to spend your money, your youngster's early education ought to be right up there after the basic necessities of family life—or perhaps even among them, according to some authorities on child development.

Another important point of view toward money is how young children look at it. Their attitudes begin much earlier than you may think.

They hear and watch what you say and do about it. They like the shape of coins, the pleasant feel, the shiny look and the jingling noise.

By three, they know it can buy things—"good" ones like candy, ice cream and toys, and others like food and clothing. They have usually learned that it's not to be put into their mouths or to be played with.

They also may already know that some children are "rich" and others "poor," although they might be a little mixed up on that point as one Rockefeller child may have been because of his few cents' allowance every week.

Among the ways you can help a preschool child learn to handle money are these:

• Provide a small allowance every week. Give it regularly, not for good behavior and not taken away for bad behavior. The size? Your decision, but 10¢ to 25¢ may be enough.

• Talk about how daddy and mother earn money, and if possible have him visit you at work.

• Let him make simple buying decisions that are important to him, a choice of a toy car or an ice cream cone, for example.

• Take him to the bank with you and explain very simply what you do there.

• Protect him from worry about money crises. Nothing is gained by sharing them with a young child, and much can be lost, like his security and faith in you.

- Let him make small purchases and return with the change, but not handle amounts of money that would upset you if they are lost.
- Encourage saving in a play bank at home, using coins that relatives might provide. Some of the allowance may sometimes be saved, of course, but the rest is for spending—wisely.
- Bring him into simple discussions about not-too-long-range family decisions, like saving for or buying a TV set.
- Help him divide a pile of pennies for presents at Christmas time, and let him share the fun of selecting and buying the gifts.

Preschool children are too young to earn money for work done at home, and should not receive pay for doing regular household jobs. Taking out the garbage, helping with the dishes, and picking up after the dog shouldn't be paid for any more than taking a bath or tying shoelaces.

Teaching a young child about money isn't easy. But we should begin early, to help prepare for how hard it is to earn and to use well.

Only by having and spending money (with your guidance) can a young child learn the differences among coins and what should and should not be done with them and other money.

The Author

Willard Abraham, recognized nationally as a leading authority on the care and training of young children, received his Ph.D. from Northwestern University.

Dr. Abraham has been a consultant for many industrial, governmental and early childhood organizations, and served as delegate to both the 1960 and 1970 White House Conferences on Children and Youth. He writes a syndicated column and has contributed numerous articles to publications such as *Today's Health* and *Family Circle*. He is the author of ten books, including *Common Sense About Gifted Children, A Time for Teaching* and *A New Look at Reading*.

Dr. Abraham has been for a number of years chairman of the Department of Special Education at Arizona State University and lives in Scottsdale with his wife and three children.